T0198168

## Get the eBook FREE!

(PDF, ePub, Kindle, and liveBook all included)

We believe that once you buy a book from us, you should be able to read it in any format we have available. To get electronic versions of this book at no additional cost to you, purchase and then register this book at the Manning website.

Go to https://www.manning.com/freebook and follow the instructions to complete your pBook registration.

## That's it!
## Thanks from Manning!

*Design for the Mind*

# Design for the Mind

### SEVEN PSYCHOLOGICAL PRINCIPLES OF PERSUASIVE DESIGN

VICTOR S. YOCCO

MANNING

SHELTER ISLAND

For online information and ordering of this and other Manning books, please visit
www.manning.com. The publisher offers discounts on this book when ordered in quantity.
For more information, please contact

> Special Sales Department
> Manning Publications Co.
> 20 Baldwin Road
> PO Box 761
> Shelter Island, NY 11964
> Email: orders@manning.com

Manning Publications Co.
20 Baldwin Road
PO Box 761
Shelter Island, NY 11964

| | |
|---|---|
| Development editor: | Helen Stergius |
| Technical development editor: | Ryan Elston |
| Review editor: | Ozren Harlovic |
| Project editor: | Tiffany Taylor |
| Copyeditor: | Liz Welch |
| Proofreader: | Elizabeth Martin |
| Typesetter: | Marija Tudor |
| Cover designer: | Morgan Knepper |

ISBN: 9781617292958
Printed in the United States of America

*To Maxwell, Emily, and Eleanor Yocco*

# brief contents

# contents

# preface

Psychology is all around us. It's woven into everything we do. Nowhere is this more apparent than when you design products for human use. How will users engage with a product? Why do users behave the way they do? Which elements of your design are key to facilitating the behaviors you want users to engage in? Psychology helps answer these questions, guiding you to making effective design decisions. Yet psychological principles stem from academic research and literature, which can often be inaccessible for practitioners. I wrote this book to help you make sense of what we know about psychology and how to apply it to design.

I became familiar with many principles of psychology through my education and pre-design work history. At the time, I was learning how psychology applied to communicating environmental issues to visitors in settings like science centers and zoos. Later, I started working as a researcher with Intuitive Company (IC), a digital design and development firm. I quickly realized everything I had learned about psychological theories and research was applicable to digital settings as well, particularly the psychology of persuasion and influence.

In January 2014, I gave a presentation on the application of persuasive psychology to design to my colleagues at IC. As I gave the presentation, I felt the state known as *flow*—an immersive state of focus, full involvement, and energy that a person enters when performing an activity aligned with their passions. I knew I had stumbled across something I loved doing: teaching others the application of psychology to design. From there, I started writing about psychology and design. I wrote articles for *A List Apart, Smashing Magazine,* and *UX Booth,* and I realized there was more than enough relevant content to produce multiple books for practitioners. That's when I decided to pursue a lifelong goal of writing a book.

This book grew up alongside a baby. My wife was pregnant as I shopped my proposal, which eventually found a home at Manning Publications. I signed with

Manning on March 2, 2015, and our daughter Eleanor was born on March 7. You can see the influence of my wife's pregnancy and our newborn daughter throughout the pages of this book. I hope to someday read Eleanor, Emily, and Maxwell's books about the world and how they see it.

I've enjoyed receiving reactions from readers of the articles I've published. It's been rewarding to witness the response of my colleagues and our clients as we discuss how our designs address key psychological principles. I've learned a lot about myself and about psychology while writing *Design for the Mind*. I'll continue to write articles, perhaps shifting my focus some to cover content related to what I do on a daily basis—user experience research. I hope you'll benefit as much from reading this book as I have from writing it, and that the book provides you with insight that will make your design more effective and help you understand why psychology matters when it comes to the products we design.

# *acknowledgments*

A lot of people were involved in bringing this book to life. From my family, I want to acknowledge my wife Deanna. Her patience and support have helped more than she will ever know. I am grateful for the love and support of Maxwell, Emily, and Eleanor Yocco. I hope the three of you always ask questions and seek answers. Evelyn Yocco, my mother, played a huge role by instilling a love for books and knowledge in my life. I wouldn't have developed an interest in writing if it weren't for her influence.

My colleagues at IC all deserve a huge thank you. You all inspire me to do my best every day. I specifically want to thank the wonderful Dr. Jes Koepfler; she saw the potential for me to be great and gave me the opportunities to do so. Thank you to Morgan Knepper, whose work graces the cover of this book. Special thanks to the research team at IC: Rob Tannen, Steve Jones, Georgia Spangenberg, Nidhi Jalwal, and Meghan Plank. They reviewed early drafts of my chapters and provided critical feedback. I owe each of you my gratitude and a cheery. Thank you Tony Daddario, a great designer who keeps me on my toes thinking about how this stuff works. And a huge thank you to Greg Picarelli, Tim McLaughlin, and Sandy Greene. The three of you have supported everything I have done at IC since day one. I couldn't ask for more.

Thanks to the book's technical peer reviewers, led by Ozren Harlovic: Timo Bredenoort, Alberto Chiesa, Noreen Dertinger, Daniel Essin, Joel Kotarski, Amit Lamba, Alan Lenton, Jason Pike, Alvin Raj, Patrick Rein, Rahul, Birnou Sébarte, Craig Smith, John Stemper, Andrew Ulrich, and Dr. Adrian Ward. Thanks also to Ryan Elston, who served as the book's technical editor.

Many folks at Manning Publications deserve credit for making this project happen. I'm thankful to Robin de Jongh, the acquisitions editor who saw enough potential in my proposal to make the case for the book, and Lynn Beighley, my initial development editor. Thank you to everyone on the Manning editorial, production, and marketing teams, including Jeff Bleiel, Toni Bowers, Candace Gillhoolley, Ozren Harlovic,

Rebecca Rinehart, Maureen Spencer, Janet Vail, Tiffany Taylor, Liz Welch, Elizabeth Martin, and Marija Tudor. A huge thank you goes to my editor, Helen Stergius: she is responsible for making this book something I am proud to have my name attached to. Finally, thank you to the publisher, Marjan Bace, who made me the offer and helped put all the pieces together to make this book happen.

# *about this book*

This book is a both a primer and a how-to on the application of key principles of psychology to design. You don't need to have a background in psychology to understand the concepts covered in this book. My purpose is to show students and practitioners of design, and those working with designers, how you can use psychology to enhance the usability of your product. If you're already familiar with psychology, this book should provide concrete examples of how to address psychological models of behavior and persuasion you might already have familiarity with in your design. For every principle, I provide multiple examples and stories on how the principle's components apply to design practitioners. I also provide a more in-depth case study of a specific digital property for each principle. Note that, with the exception of Intuitive Company, I have not had a professional relationship with any of the companies whose products I use as examples in this book.

## Who should read this book

This book is a guide to increasing users' interest and engagement with your design. You'll see how to convince users to make purchases and recommend your design to others, and how to maximize efficiency for both designers and users.

You need to include psychology and other social sciences in your design strategy if you want to create a good user experience. I wrote this book for anyone focused on digital user experience. This includes interaction and visual designers, developers, researchers, project managers, and others contributing to the conversation of good design principles. If you're currently a designer or work as a member of a design team, this book will allow you to improve the ability of your design to meet current users' needs through psychology.

Digital marketing professionals, design instructors/professors, students, and those transitioning from other fields will find value in this book as well. This book will show digital marketers how you can enhance the impact of your products' marketing through the use of psychological principles. Professors, students, and readers transitioning from other fields will learn how users' needs can be met through addressing psychological principles in a product's design.

I assume you have basic knowledge of digital design principles. I also assume you want to increase the use and usability of your designs. I make no assumptions as to your level of education or your background knowledge of psychology. I use design-focused language to explain each topic in this book.

## Roadmap

In part 1, "Introducing the application of psychology to design," you'll learn what principles the book will cover and why I chose these specific principles. I offer a comparison of a digital product designed without taking into account user psychology and another that reflects designing with user psychology in mind. Finally, I explain the difference between the type of persuasion I promote and the commonly frowned-on dark pattern and bait-and-switch type of persuasion that people often think of when they hear the word *persuasion*.

Part 2, "Why do folks act like that? Principles of behavior," covers three principles of psychology. Chapter 2 discusses planned behavior: the types of behavior that individuals knowingly engage in. Chapter 3 covers decisions people make in situations with uncertain outcomes. Academics refer to these as *risky decisions*, because outcomes often aren't guaranteed. Chapter 4 introduces the principle of motivation, ability, and trigger. I based this principle on the work of BJ Fogg and his research on persuasive technology. You'll learn that in order to maximize the likelihood of users engaging in the behavior you want them to (for example, clicking a link), you need to present them with the call to action at the right time: when they're motivated and have the ability to engage in the action.

Part 3, "Principles of influence and persuasion: not as evil as you'd think," introduces principles directly tied to influence and persuasion. Chapter 5 provides everything you need to know to begin addressing influence using research-supported techniques. Chapter 6 expands the discussion of influence into the realm of social influence. People are inherently social, and your design should reflect this. Chapter 7 focuses on how to frame communication to your users. You'll learn how to craft well-framed communication in this chapter. Chapter 8 presents a research-based model for how persuasion works. The Elaboration Likelihood Model explains that people are persuaded through deep processing of information as well as peripheral information, such as the credibility they give the source of the message. You'll learn how to address both of these methods of persuasion with your product's design.

Part 4, "User experience design: putting it all together," provides a review of the principles I've discussed and the conclusion of the book. Chapter 9 presents a case study, allowing you to practice what you've learned throughout the book. Chapter 10 shows how psychology fits into various stages of the design process, provides you with more information about research methods to help ensure that your design meets your users' needs, and gives examples of how to measure the success of incorporating psychological principles into your product's design.

## How to read this book

I wrote chapters 2 through 8 to be self-contained. You can turn to any of them and learn about the topic covered without needing the context of any previous or subsequent chapters.

Additionally, each chapter

- Provides a scenario highlighting the principle in action
- Offers some academic background highlighting research relevant to the principle covered
- Explains the principle and breaks down its major factors using digital design examples
- Presents a case study to reinforce the principle's application to design
- Contains an end-of-chapter exercise for you to practice using the principle
- Shows you how to "talk the talk" about the principle with non-experts in the field of psychology, such as clients, peers, and users
- Summarizes what was learned about the principle
- Includes an annotated list of additional resources and keywords to search online for more information

I recommend keeping the following items in mind as you read the book:

- Look for the connection between different features of your design and the principles covered.
- Think critically about your design, the assumptions you have about users, and the decisions you make to influence their behavior.
- Identify opportunities to improve how your design can use components of a principle to meet users' needs; you don't need to use every piece of every principle.
- Look for opportunities to communicate to others how you address principles of psychology in your design.
- Note opportunities for collecting data from users to complement your new knowledge of psychological principles.

## End-of-chapter exercises

I have included an end-of-chapter exercise for you to practice each of the principles covered in the book. I encourage you to participate in the book's online forum by posting your responses to each exercise. You can find threads dedicated to each chapter's exercise here: https://forums.manning.com/forums/design-for-the-mind.

## About the author

Victor Yocco, PhD, is a research director at a Philadelphia-based digital design firm. He received his PhD from The Ohio State University, where his research focused on psychology and communication in informal learning settings. Victor regularly writes and speaks on topics related to the application of psychology to design and addressing the culture of alcohol use in design and technology. He can be found at www.victoryocco.com or @victoryocco on Twitter.

# *Author Online*

Purchase of *Design for the Mind* includes free access to a private web forum run by Manning Publications where you can make comments about the book, ask technical questions, and receive help from the author and from other users. To access the forum and subscribe to it, point your web browser to https://www.manning.com/books/design-for-the-mind. This page provides information on how to get on the forum once you're registered, what kind of help is available, and the rules of conduct on the forum.

Manning's commitment to our readers is to provide a venue where a meaningful dialog between individual readers and between readers and the author can take place. It is not a commitment to any specific amount of participation on the part of the author, whose contribution to Author Online remains voluntary (and unpaid). We suggest you try asking the author some challenging questions lest his interest stray! The Author Online forum and the archives of previous discussions will be accessible from the publisher's website as long as the book is in print.

# Part 1

## Introducing the application of psychology to design

What is psychology? How can you apply psychology to design? What principles of psychology will you learn about in this book? Isn't persuasion a bad word, or even a dark art? What does it look like to design without consideration of users' psychology? I'll answer each of these questions in part 1. You'll learn what principles the book will cover, and why I chose these specific principles. I'll discuss *why* you should read this book, and *how* you should read it. I'll offer a comparison of a digital product designed without taking into account user psychology and one that was designed with user psychology in mind. I'll explain the difference between the type of persuasion I promote and the commonly frowned upon dark pattern and bait-and-switch type of persuasion that people often think of when they hear the word *persuasion*. Finally, I'll provide a cheat sheet to help you decide whether to read the book from cover to cover, or immediately go to the principles that are most relevant to your product.

# Meeting users' needs: including psychology in design 1

**This chapter covers**
- Why you should read this book
- Knowledge and skills you'll gain
- Effective UX design using psychological principles

If I told you that after you invest a few hours of your time you can learn things that will enhance the rest of your design career, you'd probably demand that I tell you how, right now. That's the purpose of this book. This book focuses on *psychology*, the study of the mental processes that lead to human behavior, and how you can apply it to design. Good design reflects users' psychology as a way of meeting their needs. As a product designer, you want to understand psychological principles so that you can adapt your product to new technologies or social contexts without relearning concrete design patterns. Whether you want to tweak an existing website to make it more intuitive or build a digital experience aligned with how users make decisions, this book is the tool for you. You'll learn principles of psychology that allow your design to

- Create or change user behavior
- Account for users making quick decisions
- Present users with a call to action at the right time

- Shape users' positive attitudes toward your design
- Incorporate social elements and interactions to influence users
- Persuade users to engage deeper with your product
- Communicate meaningfully with users about your design

Ultimately, you'll create happier users when you account for principles of psychology in your design (figure 1.1).

Figure 1.1   You reap the benefits of happy users when you incorporate psychology into your design.

## 1.1    *Principles included in this book*

This book covers seven commonly accepted principles of psychology:

- Planned behavior
- Prospect theory and heuristics
- Fogg's behavior model
- Influence
- Social influence
- Framing communication
- Persuasion

I've broken the principles into two sections.

### 1.1.1    *Design to create and change behaviors*

This section covers three principles explaining how to create usable designs that encourage users and their peers to successfully engage with your product. This includes simple user behaviors such as reading or posting a message, as well as more complex behaviors such as making a purchase or using your product to manage their finances. These topics are covered in part 2:

- *Chapter 2, "Designing for regular use: addressing planned behavior"*—This chapter shows how to make users want to engage with your product to meet their needs.
- *Chapter 3, "Risky decisions and mental shortcuts"*—This chapter examines how you can design to reduce users' mental effort, making you the go-to product for these users.
- *Chapter 4, "Motivation, ability, and trigger—boom!"*—This chapter looks at how and when to present users with the opportunity to use your product.

### 1.1.2    *Design for influence and persuasion*

Sometimes users need that extra push to use your product. This section covers four principles explaining how individuals are persuaded and influenced. These principles, covered in part 3, involve elements of design that change or reinforce users' attitudes toward your product:

- *Chapter 5, "Influence: getting people to like and use your product"*—Influence helps promote use of your product by nonusers and increase use by current users.
- *Chapter 6, "Using family, friends, and social networks to influence users"*—Social influence determines how users decide to follow what others do, and how you can design to facilitate social experiences that will increase use of your product.
- *Chapter 7, "It's not what you say; it's how you say it!"*—Framing communication will allow you to deliver a powerful and effective message to motivate users to engage in specific behaviors.
- *Chapter 8, "Persuasion: The deadliest art"*—Principles of persuasion govern how users receive and pay attention to the information you present.

## 1.2 Criteria for inclusion in this book

You can apply many legitimate principles of psychology to design. I've filtered these to those principles that will quickly serve your needs as a member of a design team.

Each principle is

- Taught in graduate-level psychology courses
- Cited hundreds of times in academic literature
- Simple to understand
- Relevant to design

### 1.2.1 Taught in graduate school

Academics constantly subject psychological principles to scrutiny. Therefore, one important benchmark I used was that these principles are currently taught in graduate-level psychology courses at accredited universities. This means that these principles are valid for designing and conducting research.

### 1.2.2 Citations: a popularity contest

Citations are the most critical factor in the survival of a principle of psychology. Researchers continue to examine each principle covered in this book. I encourage you to look into the additional resources I provide at the end of each chapter.

### 1.2.3 Simplicity

Just as many designers think a simple design is more aesthetically pleasing and functional than an overly complicated one, the same holds true for principles of psychology. Simplicity is a hallmark of a good psychological principle.

### 1.2.4 Relevant to design

I explore the usefulness of each principle as applied to your work on a design team. I've read numerous books and dozens of articles on each principle I've included. I work on design teams to incorporate these principles into designs our clients and their users find useful and usable.

## 1.3    Why you should read this book

You'll quickly gain knowledge and skills to improve how your design addresses users' psychological characteristics and encourages increased use of your design. I'll discuss the effectiveness of including psychology in your design-related conversations with peers and clients. You'll learn how to address basic human behavior in your design. Your knowledge of what makes people tick will enable you to make design decisions leading to the outcomes you desire (more clicks, more likes, and more purchases).

### 1.3.1    You'll gain knowledge

You'll be able to make decisions backed by science once you've read this book. You'll have more than basic knowledge of how relevant psychological principles apply to digital design.

I make a number of recommendations for collecting data throughout the book. I also provide guidance on questions you should ask potential users. I believe this is necessary to empower you as a reader and to show real-life application of the concepts covered.

### 1.3.2    You'll learn how to think like your users

You'll understand what mental processes lead to the decisions people make. You can apply this knowledge to make sure your design meets the needs of your users, as well as identify areas where your design isn't meeting those needs. You can address these areas to improve the performance of your design. You'll understand where users might struggle with a design and how to address this issue.

### 1.3.3    You'll learn to communicate the needs of users

After reading this book, you'll be able to better contribute to design team discussions and processes. You'll learn principles of psychology that will allow you to discuss with your team, your clients, and your peers why your design is effective, or what needs to be done to create an effective design. You'll have the ability to do this from the perspective of a user.

This book will enable you to contribute more to, and better understand, the conversation on user research and your design.

## 1.4    What this book won't teach you

This isn't a research methods book. I won't teach you how to conduct research to make your design decisions. I advocate having trained researchers collect data. You'll obtain higher quality data and better recommendations from a trained researcher. If you aren't a trained researcher, you can benefit from knowing what types of questions researchers should ask and whom they should ask.

This book also doesn't

- Provide standardized visual design requirements; I still want you to be creative.
- Teach you dirty design tricks (such as dark patterns).
- Teach you to be a designer. I'm going to give you what you need to critically think about the application of principles of psychology to your design, but I won't show you how to design.
- Specify which principle of psychology is exactly right for your design (but I'll give you plenty to choose from; try them all).

## 1.5   Addressing psychology enhances usability

This book focuses on psychology, the study of the mental processes that lead to human attitudes and behavior. I've also mixed in a bit of behavioral economics and sociology. These social sciences seek to explain the how and why behind individual and group behavior. Good design accounts for the behavior and mental processes of users. The principles in this book will get people to use your product the way you intended and recommend it to others, and will increase use of your product.

### 1.5.1   What designing without psychology looks like

ECSI, a student loan servicing company, provides an example of a design that reflects no recognizable thought to human psychology. The ECSI portal dashboard (figure 1.2) page creates more questions than answers when users land on it. For example, why does ECSI provide four different payment links: credit card, e-check, direct, and international? Why doesn't it provide visual cues as to what users should do? Why does the portal have a navigation category dedicated to Other that has only one option? Why is there so much open space when ECSI crushes the links together as tightly as possible? Why doesn't the page state the user's name, account number, or balance once logged in? Why doesn't ECSI convey a sense of security to users? I feel confused and out of control on this site and I'm sure others do too.

You'll realize after reading this book that the site isn't accounting for psychology-backed usability issues, including

- Perceived control
- Immediate guidance
- Personalization
- Perceived security (third-party seals, antivirus status)
- Familiar layout for a customer portal (for example, informational dashboard landing)
- Persuasive elements of any type

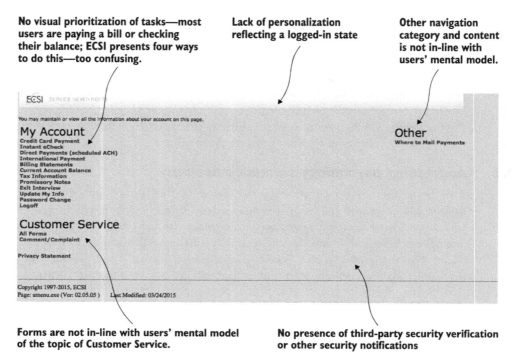

No visual prioritization of tasks—most users are paying a bill or checking their balance; ECSI presents four ways to do this—too confusing.

Lack of personalization reflecting a logged-in state

Other navigation category and content is not in-line with users' mental model.

Forms are not in-line with users' mental model of the topic of Customer Service.

No presence of third-party security verification or other security notifications

**Figure 1.2   ECSI doesn't account for psychological principles of any type on the portal landing page.**

### 1.5.2   *What designing with psychology looks like*

Aqua, my water provider, does a much better job acknowledging principles of psychology in its customer portal. The Aqua customer portal (figure 1.3) visually guides me to the most frequently used (and most important to Aqua) options of making a payment and setting up auto draft (not displayed, but it appears in the Payments navigation category). I feel in control thanks to the personalized greeting and clear navigation. I feel secure seeing the recent activity feed and third-party seal. I don't love paying any bill, but I don't mind paying my water bill or using Aqua's online portal to check my balance. I'll cover the importance of control, simplicity, personalization, and security as psychological principles in later chapters.

Both businesses offer a payment portal with nearly identical functionality. But users will view the ECSI portal as confusing, with poor workflows and no guidance on what tasks are located where, and lacking a logical layout. Users will view Aqua as a business that values their time and wants them to succeed in tasks related to managing their account. Aqua has done this through effective use of principles of psychology.

Digital experiences that fail to account for psychology aren't always as obvious as the ECSI portal. How can you avoid designing experiences like ECSI's? Psychological principles provide a map to guide your process. They help explain the what and why behind your design.

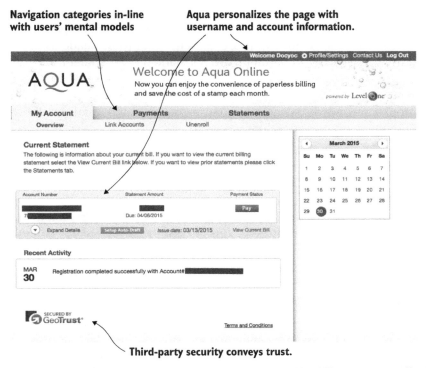

**Figure 1.3   Aqua accounts for principles of psychology, making bill payment easy if not fun.**

## 1.6   *And now, a passionate word on persuasion*

This book covers a number of principles focused on persuading users. I'm unabashedly pro persuasive design. I think persuasion has a bad rap—but I understand why. The word typically conjures up images of a smooth-talking salesperson, someone who doesn't have your best interests in mind. In design, this can mean trickery and deceit through dark patterns. I'm not writing a book about that kind of persuasion. I'm writing about making your experience persuasive by making it easy to use, by using psychology to improve your design, and by getting people to engage in behaviors they were already considering. I'm writing about being persuasive in the way that Amazon.com persuades users with recommendations, options, and a usable experience. I'm writing about being persuasive like Google, with targeted advertising, personalization, and an extensive lineup of useful free apps; persuasive like Apple, with simple, appealing design, future-focused functionality, and a cult following.

The truth about persuasion is much more benign.[1] Persuasion is part of our everyday lives, whether or not we acknowledge it. People need to be persuaded, not

---

[1]   I stated in my July 2014 article on persuasion in *A List Apart*, "Utilizing dark patterns or tricking a user into doing something they wouldn't otherwise do is not persuasion. It's being an asshole." See http://mng.bz/n6nK.

because they're dumb or should be tricked, but because most people don't have the time to waste mental resources on making many of life's less complicated decisions. You also know that your competitors are actively trying to persuade users to try their product. In other words, if you don't try to persuade people, someone else gladly will.

Figure 1.4 is an example of what I consider dirty persuasion—the kind that gives everyday persuasion a bad name. This "article" lives as a paid sponsor link on a number of popular (assumedly reputable) mainstream news and weather websites. Notice some of the shady persuasive techniques used:

- The article is an advertisement masked as journalism—many readers won't notice the small and confusing word "advertorial" featured in the upper-right corner. Instead, the ad reads like breaking news, exposing the reader to an inside government secret on how they can get out of debt.
- Additional links, similarly attention-grabbing, yet likely false, tell the reader the "secret" of getting out of debt. I'm guessing that secret only comes after the reader completes a form and possibly provides a payment.
- Although the article suggests mortgage rates have gone down, they blind the rates, asking users to click Check Rates. I didn't want to find out what would happen to my computer if I did click the link.

I'm left assuming (possibly incorrectly) that this is a more modern version of bait and switch or postal fraud. The target audience seems to be the elderly or those still under the impression that "It must be true because the internet says so." I'm disappointed sites like this exist and are able to advertise through (supposedly) reputable sites.

You'll learn much more about positive persuasion as you read this book. You get the point, and I'm done talking up persuasion.

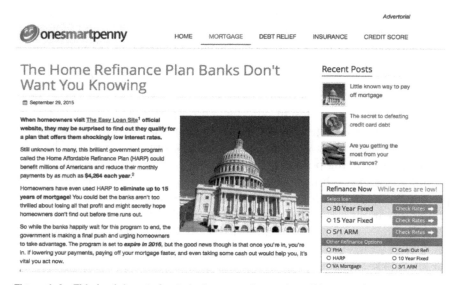

**Figure 1.4  This book is not about shady persuasion such as this example.**

## 1.7    *Talking the talk: conversations about psychology*

When you understand principles of psychology, you enhance your ability to explain the underlying rationale of your design. But you need to do this without sounding pompous. Remember, most people won't be as well versed in these principles as you. I'll provide examples throughout the book of how you might subtly discuss each principle with clients, peers, or users. Your ability to effectively communicate these concepts will put you ahead of the competition.

Let's compare how two designers, Brainy and Dr. K., separately discuss with a potential client why incorporating social interactions into their design should be effective. Brainy doesn't know much about psychological principles related to design, whereas Dr. K became familiar with the components of social identity (covered in chapter 6) in preparation for the project.

**Brainy:** "Our design recommendations will focus on the act of liking. Everyone likes Facebook because they get to see what their friends are doing and if they like what they see, they press the Like button. So we are going to strategically place Like buttons all around your product so people can Like things too. It's going to be a real hit!"

**Dr. K.:** "Our design will allow your users to see what other users with similar interests are doing with your product. We know from psychological research that people look at what others are doing and compare themselves to those people. Your product now facilitates the creation of groups of like-minded users. They'll be able to see how others use your product, trade tips on using your product, and create a broader word-of-mouth effort around your product."

It should be obvious who impressed the client more. Dr. K clearly made a better attempt to inform her design beyond generic impressions from observing behavior on Facebook. You too can easily start to talk the talk of principles of psychology, without sounding condescending or obtuse (fun word).

## 1.8    *Summary*

- Principles of psychology are core to UX and user-focused design, so use them often.
- Principles of psychology serve to explain why and how people choose to engage in certain behaviors.
- Understanding the importance of principles of psychology will enhance your design and increase user happiness.
- Users will notice if your design ignores psychology; they won't use your product.
- You should proactively think about how each principle might apply to your design.
- Psychological principles provide a blueprint for your design—you can use part or all of a psychological principle and you can mix principles within your design to create the best product possible.

- Persuasion is *not* a dirty word; this book covers persuasive techniques meant to create a better user experience, not trick users into doing something they don't want to do.

## 1.9    *Cheat sheet*

Although I fully expect you'll read this book from cover to cover, I want to be respectful of your time. You can use the following questions to help guide you to the most appropriate principle for your product. You can choose to read the chapters I identify here first, and then cover the rest of the principles as you find the time:

- What are you trying to accomplish beyond usability?
  - All of the principles in this book cover this.
- Is your experience social?
  - Start with something from chapter 6 on social identity and social influence.
- Is your experience intimate or personal?
  - Start with chapter 5 on influence or chapter 8 on persuasion, complemented with framing from chapter 7.
- Are you designing for frequent behaviors such as personal banking or checking the weather forecast?
  - Start with chapter 2 on planned behavior and chapter 4 on presenting effective triggers.
- Are you designing for spontaneous behaviors such as eating out in an unfamiliar neighborhood, or signing up for a monthly newsletter while users are browsing your website for the first time?
  - Start with chapter 3 on risky decisions and chapter 4 on presenting effective triggers.
- Does your experience sell things?
  - Start with chapter 5 on influence and chapter 8 on persuasion.
- Does your experience promote a certain attitude toward a political or environmental issue?
  - Start with chapter 2 on planned behavior.
- Is your experience health or fitness related?
  - Start with chapter 2 on planned behavior, chapter 4 on presenting effective triggers, and chapter 7 on framing communication.

# Part 2

# *Why do folks act like that?*
# *Principles of behavior*

Psychology researchers have long attempted to identify the factors that lead to a behavior. In this part of the book, you'll learn about three principles. Each provides a blueprint for addressing factors leading to both planned and more spontaneous (risky) behaviors.

Chapter 2 covers planned behavior, the types of behavior that individuals knowingly engage in. This includes major and infrequent decisions such as purchasing a new home, as well as minor decisions such as which news website a user is likely to seek information from. You'll learn how to design for each of the pieces researchers have identified as leading to planned behavior.

Chapter 3 covers decisions people make under situations with uncertain outcomes. Academics refer to these as risky decisions, as outcomes are often not guaranteed. You'll learn about the processes of editing and evaluation that lead to decision making. I'll also cover heuristics, or mental shortcuts, that people often use to make decisions when information is lacking.

Chapter 4 introduces the principle of motivation, ability, and trigger. I based this principle off the work of B.J. Fogg and his research on persuasive technology. You'll learn that in order to maximize the likelihood of users engaging in the behavior you want them to (for example, clicking a link) you need to present them with the call to action at the right time: when they're motivated and have the ability to engage in the action. I'll cover examples of how you can address this in your design, highlighting the application of this principle to mobile design.

# Designing for regular use: addressing planned behavior

Daniel is a designer at a bank working on a new personal financial management application. He used his knowledge of planned behavior to design the app to account for many beliefs he knows the bank's customers have: they want to save money, they believe the bank provides reliable financial advice, and they believe personal financial management applications give them more control over their financial decisions. Daniel and his product team at the bank also make the app available free of charge for those holding an account with the bank. Daniel uses this information to craft an email informing bank customers of the new application and asking them to download the application to their smartphone or tablet.

Anita receives the email letting her know there is a new mobile application dedicated to personal financial management. She reads the message and then downloads the app to her phone. The principle of planned behavior (figure 2.1)

15

explains her positive response to the email: Anita believes saving money and managing her finances accurately is a good thing. Anita believes her colleagues, friends, and relatives use similar financial management apps. She believes the application itself is designed to give her more insight and control over her finances. She also believes she has final say over whether she downloads the free app.

People have a reason for many of the things they do. *Your* goal is to understand your users' way of thinking about their regularly planned behaviors. What do you as a designer need to do to help users meet their behavioral goals?

Maybe you want to understand your users' goal of managing and paying their monthly electric bills online. You also want to understand how users expect to interact with a digital bill pay system to manage bills within an online banking portal. What are users' expectations related to the experience? How much time do they expect to invest managing their bills? What other options for account management will they need available online? How often will they engage in banking tasks along with paying their electric bill?

What makes your users choose to engage in a behavior (or not) can elevate how your design meets their needs and expectations, as well as how you might use your design to help reinforce or change user behaviors around your product.

## 2.1    Introduction

Your users' decision to engage in a behavior is the outcome of their beliefs and attitudes toward the behavior, whether they think that behavior is socially acceptable, and

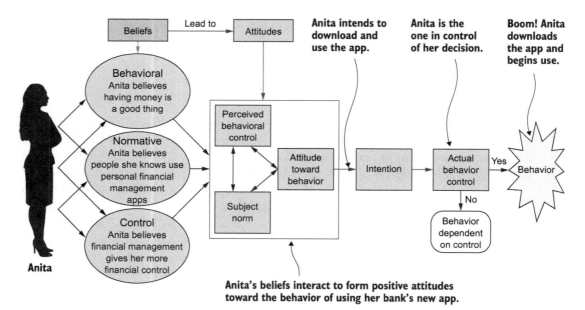

**Figure 2.1   Components of planned behavior. Beliefs lead to attitudes, which create intention and then behavior, if the individual is in control of the behavior.**

if they think they have the power to make the final decision about the behavior. Beliefs and attitudes do a funky dance together (figure 2.1), leading to intention. Intention links directly to behavior. If you account for these factors in your design, you should be able to predict with relative accuracy what a user's end behavior will be: use of your product.

### 2.1.1 Brief academic background

Academics consider predicting behavior the holy grail of psychology research. If we can determine what causes people to behave in certain ways, we can then effectively develop programs to cause or change behavior. In 1985, Icek Ajzen, a University of Massachusetts professor, surveyed the psychological literature on behavior. He concluded that people purposely engage in a behavior to achieve a specific outcome. For example, I purposely open my laptop with the intention of writing a new chapter in this book. We can apply this to any product ever designed. People purposely use a product with an intended outcome in mind.

Ajzen wanted to understand more about what led to people's behaviors. He set forth with a number of his colleagues to engage in studies to determine the main factors contributing to planned behavior. As shown in table 2.1, the researchers concluded that three main factors lead to the intention of an individual to engage in behavior:

- *Behavioral outcome beliefs*—People have beliefs as to whether a behavior will have a good or a bad outcome. The researchers studied a group of women's use of birth control. All of the women believed that taking a birth control pill had potential negative side effects (such as weight gain or being more likely to develop blood clots). The researchers found that women with beliefs that taking an oral contraceptive had more severe negative side effects were less likely to take it. Their beliefs about the outcome of the behavior of taking birth control pills led to their not taking them.
- *Normative beliefs*—People look around at what others believe about a behavior as a reference for whether they should engage in a behavior. Using the birth control research example, the researchers found that women taking birth control pills were more likely to use them if they felt it was a behavior supported by their significant others and their doctors. They looked to these others for shaping their behavior of taking the contraceptive.
- *Control beliefs*—People's perception of control influences whether they'll engage in a behavior. People are more likely to engage in behaviors they feel control over, or that are easy to engage in. Ajzen's studies found that people who feel more control over behaviors such as exercising or hunting are more likely to engage in these behaviors. For example, Ajzen found participants who rated the act of hunting as difficult were less likely to express an intention to engage in hunting.

Many public health organizations and public health campaigns have used the components from planned behavior to shape their programs. For example, the National Highway Traffic Safety Association (NHTSA) attempts to address behavior, normative, and control beliefs in their program to reduce drunk driving. They address behavioral beliefs by funding increased law enforcement dedicated to pulling over potential drunk drivers. This addresses behavior beliefs by increasing the belief that the outcome of drinking and driving is negative—you'll be arrested. NHTSA funds advertising meant to shift the social norm; the ads highlight that our society frowns on drinking and driving. Control beliefs are addressed through programs that educate bar owners not to overserve patrons, and to provide vouchers for free or low-cost cab rides home for people who've had too much to drink. This emphasizes that bartenders are in control over stopping service to someone who is drunk, and individuals who've had too much have options for an alternative ride home. The United States has seen a steady decrease in drinking and driving deaths in the years NHTSA has been funding these programs.

Table 2.1  Planned behavior's beliefs and outcomes

| Type of belief | Definition | Outcome of belief | Applied definition |
| --- | --- | --- | --- |
| Behavioral | Users' beliefs related to the outcome of a behavior—is the outcome good or bad? | Attitude toward a specific behavior | Do your users feel positive or negative toward using your design? |
| Normative | Users' beliefs about the expectations of others toward a behavior—is the behavior socially acceptable? | Subjective norm | Do users think other people they know and like are using your design? |
| Control | Users' beliefs about who is in charge of engaging in a behavior—can people engage in the behavior by choice? | Perceived behavioral control | Do users think your design gives them more control over a behavior, and do they feel in control of choosing to use your design? |

### A few words on beliefs

Belief is a heady topic. Individuals form, shape, and reinforce beliefs through a lifetime of experiences. Beliefs are diverse (think religion or technology), and no belief is incorrect. I respect your beliefs; please respect your users' beliefs.

Planned behavior doesn't discriminate between a belief toward religion and one toward the use of color in wireframes. The concepts apply to each situation equally. That said, you have a much greater likelihood of influencing someone's positive or negative belief toward your hair care product than you do toward their religion.

## 2.2   *Key concepts of planned behavior*

Researchers use planned behavior to explain behaviors from health-related ones, such as quitting smoking and losing weight, to consumer behaviors, such as online shopping and use of social networking sites.

Let's review the components of planned behavior from a design practitioner viewpoint. Cynthia is considering purchasing a new laptop. Her current laptop is outdated, runs slowly, and often encounters errors with incompatible software. Cynthia has behavioral, normative, and control beliefs relating to the purchase of a laptop. We'll follow Cynthia as she mulls her decision to purchase a new laptop.

### 2.2.1 People want a positive outcome

*Behavior beliefs* are what people think will happen when they do something. In the split second the individual thinks about this, she forms her *attitude* toward the behavior. Is buying a new laptop good, bad, or neutral? Attitudes are based on the underlying beliefs. If the benefits of faster speed and portability outweigh the expense of the laptop, it's likely an individual will develop a positive attitude toward the purchase.

Cynthia holds certain beliefs about the behavior of purchasing a new laptop. She believes a new laptop will

- Cure the errors and slow speed she experiences with her current laptop (positive)
- Provide her with increased productivity (positive)
- Make her life better (positive)
- Cost her money (negative)

Cynthia's positive beliefs outweigh her negative beliefs about owning a new laptop, which in turn creates a positive attitude about the behavior of purchasing a new laptop.

Cynthia also has positive beliefs about using websites such as Amazon.com (figure 2.2) to search for the best deal on the products she wants to buy. She believes that Amazon

- Provides accurate product details (positive)
- Has competitive pricing with other options (positive)
- Provides guidance through user ratings (positive)

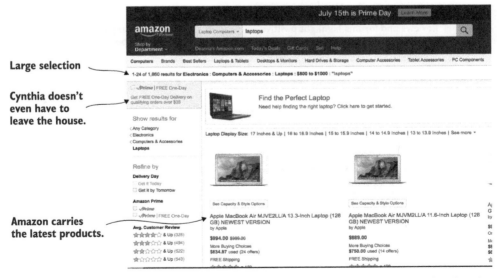

**Figure 2.2   Amazon users believe the website provides them with the products they need at the price they want.**

Therefore, she has a positive attitude about the specific behavior of shopping for a laptop on Amazon.com.

### 2.2.2    People want to know what others are doing

*Normative beliefs* are the expectations people think others hold toward a behavior. This leads to the formation of *subjective norms*, or how the individual feels others judge the behavior. Without norms, we wouldn't have taboos. The specific norm an individual forms is dependent on the group whose opinion is more relevant to the individual for the specific behavior. These normative beliefs are part of the equation when an individual is considering engaging in a behavior.

Cynthia is still thinking about purchasing a laptop. Although she believes purchasing a laptop is a good thing, she also knows some of her friends and family members frown on frivolous purchases. These people would tell her that if her current laptop is functional, it's good enough.

Cynthia looks around and realizes

- Many of her family members don't own laptops (a new laptop isn't a social norm).
- Some of her family members own laptops that are very old (a new laptop isn't a social norm).
- A few family members have new laptops (a new laptop is a social norm).
- Most of her friends use older laptops (a new laptop isn't a social norm).

Cynthia's normative beliefs are that not everyone she associates with thinks it's a good thing to own a new laptop. She thinks that others she knows would have negative attitudes toward purchasing a new laptop. Therefore, she doesn't consider owning a new laptop a subjective norm.

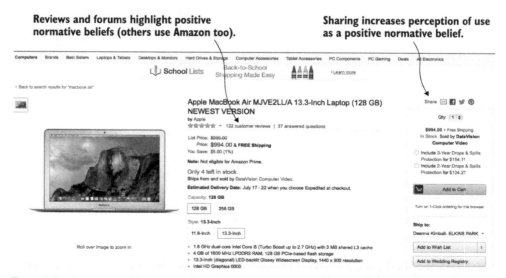

**Figure 2.3    Amazon provides customer product reviews and opportunities for community members to ask and answer questions, increasing the perception that using Amazon is a social norm.**

Cynthia also knows that many of her friends and family members use Amazon to find the best price on products, often posting reviews of what they purchase on the website (figure 2.3). Using Amazon to make a purchase is a subjective norm in her social groups.

### 2.2.3  *People want control*

*Control beliefs* reflect individuals' thoughts on whom or where the power to choose to engage in a behavior lies. What barriers must be overcome? What makes accomplishing the behavior easier? *Perceived behavioral control* is the level of ease an individual assigns to completing the behavior. Is it up to the individual whether she can purchase a new laptop, or does she feel she needs to ask for her parents' permission? If so, do her parents hold the final say in whether she can make the purchase? Many people blame their behavior on something or someone else being in control. Think about that as you consider how to design for behavior. How can you give users a greater sense of control?

Cynthia believes she has final say in whether she will purchase the laptop. She considers that she

- Has a job (she's in control)
- Has the money for the computer (she's in control)
- Can easily find a great deal using the internet to research prices (she's in control)

Cynthia believes it'll be easy for her to accomplish the task of purchasing a new laptop, which in turn leads to her perception that she's the one in control of the decision. It'd be a different story if she had to borrow money or ask for her parents' permission, but she doesn't.

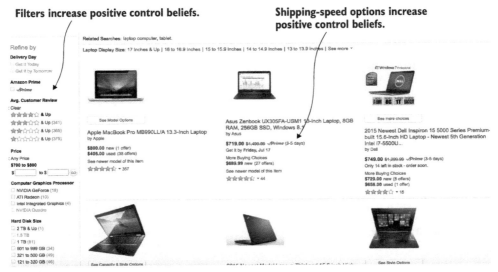

**Figure 2.4**  **Amazon's filtering features and purchasing options provide users with a greater sense of control.**

Amazon increases Cynthia's feeling of control (figure 2.4) over her purchasing decisions. Amazon allows Cynthia to

- Filter for the type of features she wants and the price range she can afford
- Shop any time of day or night
- Save and compare her favorites
- Apply for an interest-free term credit line at checkout, removing the potential barrier of cost controlling some users' purchase of a computer

### 2.2.4 People often intend to engage in a behavior

Users don't always do something just because they say they will. *Intention* is whether a person intends to engage in a behavior—yes or no. Many people can become distracted or feel they need more time to consider making a decision.

As Cynthia is browsing computers, she realizes she needs a little more time to save the money for the purchase. She intends to buy a new laptop but wants to wait until her next pay period. Amazon accounts for her future intention by allowing her to save the laptop she wants in a cart for her to come back to quickly view and purchase in the future (figure 2.5).

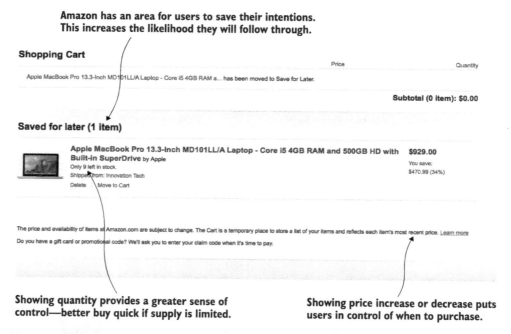

**Figure 2.5**   Amazon allows users to express intention and save a product in their cart for a later purchase.

## 2.3    *How to design for users' plans*

Planned behavior provides you with insight to shape your design so that it shows users how your design fits into their plans. You're putting yourself ahead in the game if your design addresses at least one of these factors. The following sections explain how your design can show users why they should plan to use your product through behavior, normative, and control beliefs.

### 2.3.1    *Design for positive outcomes of using your design*

You want to show users clearly how they'll benefit from using what you've designed. If most potential users see value in the outcome of using your product, your life as a designer will be much easier.

For example, the Checkout 51 app (figure 2.6) allows users to save money on groceries. Users make purchases and scan their receipts. The app clearly displays what deals are available and how much money users will save. Users develop a favorable attitude toward the behavior of using Checkout 51 once they realize it facilitates the positive outcome of saving money on everyday purchases.

**Figure 2.6    Checkout 51 takes advantage of users' beliefs that saving money is good.**

Checkout 51 and similar apps are especially appealing to users who already have beliefs that mobile technology is helpful in facilitating tasks and the attitude that using mobile technology is simple. You should align your design with the platform your potential users are most comfortable with and that makes the most sense. You wouldn't want to create a restaurant-finding application that's designed for optimal use on a home computer. Many of your users are likely to be mobile when using the app.

Let's say you're designing a discount hotel booking application (think Hotels.com). Your goal is to create a product that will allow users to save money using your application.

### WHAT USERS LIKE ABOUT YOUR APPLICATION

Users may have a number of potential positive behavior beliefs about using your discount hotel booking application, including:

- Technology makes booking a hotel faster.
- You save money booking a hotel on a discount website.
- Individual hotel websites are cumbersome to navigate.
- A competing discount hotel website is hard to use or outdated.

Individuals holding these beliefs will be more likely to hold a positive attitude toward the behavior of using your product to book a room. You need to make sure your design follows through and meets these beliefs.

### WHAT USERS DON'T LIKE ABOUT YOUR APPLICATION

You might also find a number of negative beliefs about using a discount hotel application in the same population:

- New websites and applications are difficult to learn how to use.
- Hotel discount sites don't really save you money.
- Only one hotel chain has properties worth staying at.
- A competing discount hotel website does a better job than yours.

Individuals holding these beliefs are likely to hold negative attitudes toward trying your product. You'll need to show these potential users that their negative beliefs don't apply to your application.

### SHOW USERS YOU HAVE A SUPERIOR PRODUCT

It's possible that individuals will hold both positive and negative beliefs about using your product. The more strongly held belief will win out in determining the direction (positive or negative) of the attitude toward your product.

Using our hotel example, you might find that many users hold both the *positive* belief that using your application to book a room will save them money and the conflicting *negative* belief that technology is difficult to learn. Some users might feel that saving money holds greater weight than the frustration of learning a new application, leading to a positive attitude toward your product. Other potential users might be so overwhelmed thinking about learning a new product that they're unable to justify learning to save money (negative attitude). If your design can show that learning the technology is easier than the user expects, bonus points for you!

## HOW TO DESIGN FOR POSITIVE OUTCOMES

First, you need to define what you want people to believe about the behavior of using your product. These are probably in line with what I listed earlier: that your application saves time and money, and is better than competing options. You also want potential users to believe that your application is easy to learn.

You can do the following:

- Focus on efficiency when designing workflows
- Allow users to save favorite hotels and destinations
- Allow users to save settings, including payment methods
- Provide in-line validation on forms
- Provide tool tips next to form fields
- Use friendly terminology for field labels
- Conduct usability testing to uncover areas of confusion and validate design choices
- Iterate on your design to address areas of confusion
- Provide detailed FAQs to address areas of confusion
- Beta test your product with current users of your competitors' products
- Incorporate their recommendations in your full release
- Find out what works and what doesn't work for users of your competitors' products

You can validate positive attitudes by showing users they will indeed save money using your site. You should highlight this as it makes sense throughout the experience. Consider showing users what they're saving over face value, showing users the amount they've saved over a certain time using your site, and offering special sales for registered users. You should avoid going overboard and focusing only on the cost savings of using your design; you want to highlight other benefits such as time saved or ease of use as well.

For users overwhelmed with learning new applications, you should create the most usable experience possible. This includes iterating on your design using feedback from select individuals holding this belief, and creating a "lite" version of your application—one with fewer options that seems less intimidating to those unfamiliar with similar applications.

Focus on addressing behavioral beliefs that can be changed, or focus on creating new beliefs. For example, I don't advise attempting to change someone's preferred hotel. Instead, I recommend showing users your site will allow them to book their favorite hotel. Can your product complement the hotel website in some way? Can you combine additional features, such as car rental and flight reservations, that would create the beliefs that using your product saves time and gives them more control over booking on individual sites for flight, car, and hotel?

There's no one-size-fits-all solution when designing for beliefs. How you solve the problem will be what sets your product apart. What are you doing to ensure that current and potential users have positive beliefs and attitudes about the use of your product? If you can't answer that question, you have a problem.

### 2.3.2    Make your design socially acceptable

Applications like OverDrive (figure 2.7) take advantage of the existing behaviors that people check out library books and that people use e-readers or their phones to read books. You don't have to convince users your design is socially acceptable when it aligns with something people are already doing.

Accessing a library is in line with the normative belief that people borrow and read books from libraries; users must be patrons to access books.

OverDrive takes advantage of a behavior becoming a positive normative belief for many people: using an e-reader.

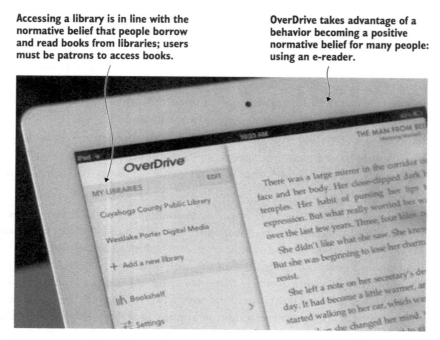

**Figure 2.7    OverDrive takes advantage of communities holding positive normative beliefs toward borrowing library books and using e-readers/smartphones to read them.**

You can also design for interactions that show users others they know are using your product. Allowing users to share using social channels (figure 2.8) helps support normative beliefs that use of a product is socially acceptable.

You need to understand how your users view the world around them. Who do they consider influential in their lives? How do they perceive their friends, family members, and colleagues feel about the product you're designing?

Sharing and other social components create a perception that others have positive subjective norms about using a product.

Always allow users many ways to share; not everyone uses the same social media tools.

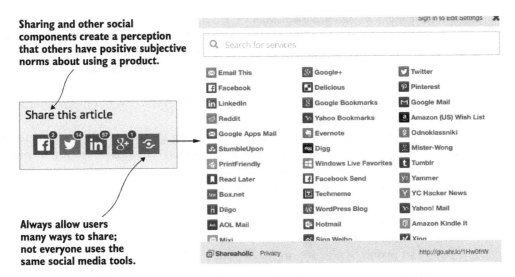

**Figure 2.8** Allowing users to share information creates a deeper perception of positive normative beliefs about use of your product.

## WHO DO YOUR USERS LOOK TO FOR GUIDANCE?

Normative beliefs serve as a compass for guiding individuals on the acceptability of certain behaviors. Using the hotel-booking application example, we find that many users have influential people they can identify who hold positive beliefs toward using a discount hotel-booking application:

- Tech-savvy peers
- Colleagues at work
- Siblings
- Business leaders
- Frequent travelers
- Actors and other personalities known for using this type of technology

The same users can identify people who hold negative beliefs toward using a discount hotel-booking application. People with negative beliefs might include

- Peers who've had negative experiences with online hotel booking
- Siblings who never travel and have heard negative stories
- Frequent travelers who prefer booking over the phone
- Frequent travelers who use professional travel arrangement services
- Pop culture icons who've made derogatory comments about hotels
- People who prefer to use non-hotel products such as Airbnb

**HOW TO DESIGN FOR SOCIAL ACCEPTANCE**

Your goal is to design experiences that users view as acceptable by their peers and the people they admire or idolize. Let's say you've identified that many potential users believe their siblings would approve of using your application and that their grandparents would disapprove of using your application. You must show potential users that the benefit of their siblings' approval is greater than the cost of engaging in an activity their grandparents disapprove of.

Once you conduct alpha testing on your design, you should recruit beta users to provide early reviews. Potential users will respond to word-of-mouth recommendations and their peers' reviews. I believe these are two of the most direct ways to encourage positive normative beliefs for using a product. This allows you to outsource the job of creating positive hype for your product and encourages people to shift negative beliefs and attitudes to positive beliefs and attitudes. I'll cover communication more in depth in later chapters.

You can promote positive norms in your marketing efforts:

- You want to highlight if a large number of people use your product.
- You should highlight if certain demographics (well-informed travelers) or types of celebrities (official booking site of arena football!) use your site.

Additional design techniques for you to engage in to promote positive subjective norms include:

- Allowing people to share their use of your product over social media
- Encouraging users to create groups and invite others to join (for example, if a group of people are vacationing together, suggest they book rooms as a group through your application)

### 2.3.3  *Giving users control*

I own both a Honda and an Acura. Honda Financial Services finances both vehicles. I'm not able to service both accounts on the Honda Financial Services website (figure 2.9). Honda Financial Services fails to provide users with an increased sense of control by requiring separate log-ins on separate sites depending on the vehicle they've financed. Offering single sign-on for these accounts would not only reduce my effort managing the accounts, it'd increase my belief that I'm in control of my car financial information when I log into one of their properties.

**Users feel less in control when they're unable to manage multiple accounts on one property.**

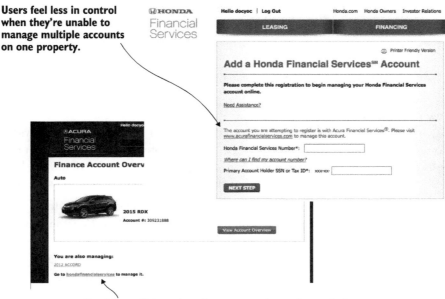

**Providing a link to the other property is a sad consolation. Users still need separate login credentials.**

**Figure 2.9   Honda Financial Services reduces users' control beliefs and perceived behavioral control for managing accounts.**

### WHAT CONTROL BELIEFS LOOK LIKE

Control beliefs are users' beliefs about factors that exist to help or prevent them from performing the behavior. This leads to perceptions of whether or not they think a behavior is easy or hard to perform. It would be incorrect to assume that all users feel they're in control of using your application.

Your hotel application's design team might investigate and find that users have the following relevant positive control beliefs:

- Booking applications allow users to choose the best option (prices and rooms) for them.
- Booking applications put users in a position of power when looking for hotel rooms.
- Online applications can be accessed from anywhere.
- Individuals get to choose when and where they use an online booking application.

Your team might investigate and find that users have the following negative control beliefs:

- Everyday people don't have access to good hotel deals.
- You have to be a frequent traveler to benefit from the discounts.
- Discounted rates equal discounted quality.

- There are limited deals available—those with faster access will get the deal.
- They don't have much advance notice of travel.
- Workplace policies prevent use of third-party booking applications for work travel.
- Booking through a third party isn't guaranteed (fear of being rebooked without an option).

**HOW TO DESIGN TO GIVE USERS CONTROL**

Solving for control beliefs and perceived behavioral control is about providing education, options, and usability. You'll need to show potential users they're in control of a behavior, or how your product will give them control over a behavior. Examples of design features for a hotel application that helps convey control to users include:

- Providing suggestions from similar users that reflect user control
- Designing filters that give users a sense of control and customization over the experience
- Comparing other sites and offline booking rates to show savings
- Allowing the option to rebook at a lower price if one is found

### 2.3.4   *Understanding who's in charge of the behavior*

An individual might want to engage in a behavior—let's say buying that laptop—but they aren't truly in control. Can you think of some times this might happen? Here are some examples of when someone isn't in control of the final decision of their behavior:

- Children
- Institutionalized individuals (for example, incarcerated criminals)
- Someone who doesn't have access to the product
- Someone in a mentally altered state (for example, using hallucinogenic drugs)

You shouldn't design for individuals who have no control over their behavior; you design for the person controlling their behavior. I clarify the need to account for actual behavioral control in the accompanying sidebar.

Who's in charge matters to design teams because you need to make sure you're designing for an audience that is in control, or that your product removes the barriers to control. If you're selling a videogame app, your design needs to appeal to the person who makes the purchasing decision. If you make it really cool and appealing to a child, that's great, but then you're relying on the child convincing the parent to make the purchase. You should try to design to influence the parent to want to purchase it for the child. Make it easy for a parent to purchase your product, make the parent aware that other parents just like them are buying your product for their kids, and give them an easy way to access your product.

Users want increased control wherever possible. Parents appreciate designs that include the ability to modify control or assign permissions: for example, blocking certain websites from certain users, preventing certain users from making purchases, or limiting the amount of a purchase a user can make. In the same way, Google experimented with removing control of users who were too drunk to send emails asking them to complete math questions before allowing them to send emails (an optional setting users could activate when sober if they feared sending "drunk email").

## The prisoners and the patisserie

Once upon a time, a baker had her shop next to a large prison. Every day the prison guards would stop in on their way to and from work to purchase the baker's goods. Often, the guards would bring along prisoners to purchase baked goods as well. The guards did this to reward prisoners who had done a good job, or when the prison bakery was running low on bread or cake. Prisoners outnumbered guards 5 to 1 as customers at the bakeshop.

The baker considered herself a UX baker. She was well regarded for putting the needs of her customers first. She always tested out new items on her customers, making changes until she got a recipe just right. But the baker never stopped to consider whether concepts of planned behavior might apply to her work.

One day the baker decided she would survey her customers. She wanted to make sure she was providing them with everything they wanted. She asked customers if they were happy with her selection and if they had recommendations for other pastries. For a whole week, the baker gave a paper copy of the survey to every customer to take home to complete.

The baker made some major changes to her inventory based on the survey responses. The next day, as soon as the bakery opened, a prison guard came in with 15 prisoners. To the baker's disappointment, the guard immediately escorted the prisoners back out to the van. Fearful of losing customers, the baker ran outside to ask the guard if there was a problem.

"Yes, there is a problem; we can't buy anything at your bakery," the guard replied. "Yesterday you had crème-filled donuts and chocolate-covered cupcakes. Today you have sponge cake filled with saw blades, pound cake stuffed with prepaid cell phones, and candied skeleton keys. Prisoners aren't allowed to have any of those things!"

"Oh, I see. I didn't realize the prisoners weren't able to make purchases without your permission," the baker said. "I changed my inventory based on their response to my survey."

"I'm sorry, but prisoners are not in control of what they can buy, and those items are not allowed in our prison," the guard replied, and then he backed the van out of the bakery parking lot. No one from the prison ever returned to make a purchase at the bakery.

This story highlights the importance of designing for a population that has control over their decisions. We don't often think about who doesn't have a say in what they can do. You can't design to influence something that you're unable to influence. Another benefit of using psychological principles is that it stretches our minds and makes us think about all the factors that we need to account for in our design.

### 2.3.5   *Designing for intention*

Lastly, you want your design to account for users who aren't yet ready to commit to the final decision. Say they know they want to use your product or make a purchase, but it isn't yet the right time. You have a number of options to account for user intention in your design:

- Allowing users to save a product for later purchase
- Providing "wish list" creation
- Giving users a free trial
- Linking with Pinterest, Instapaper, Pocket, or other save-for-later apps
- Providing tools for users to compare products and product features side by side
- Sending users reminders of what they've viewed or added to their cart
- Allowing users to set up notifications for when a price changes or a product becomes available

Pocket (figure 2.10) is an example of an application designed specifically to address intention. Users install the app, which then allows them to click the pocket icon to

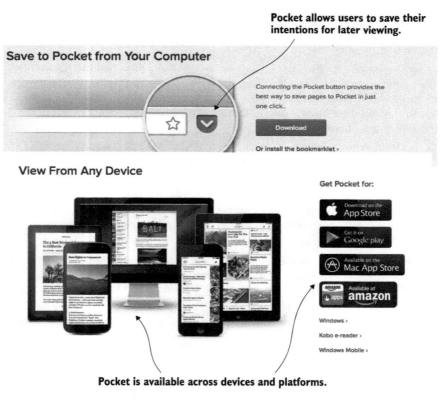

**Figure 2.10   Pocket app's design directly addresses intention; that's the purpose of the application.**

save the page they're on for later use. Users can save articles, pictures, or an item they want to purchase. Pocket allows users to keep all of the things they intend to get to eventually, in one location. Note the importance of cross-platform design for an app like Pocket. Users are likely to see something on a mobile device while they're out shopping and want to pull it up on a tablet or PC for further review when they're home. Allowing users to install an app that displays the content across platforms is critical to the value Pocket provides users.

## 2.4 *Talking the talk: conversations about planned behavior*

You risk sounding condescending or unapproachable when discussing psychological concepts and design with clients. Here are some pointers for discussing planned behavior concepts:

- *Discussing behavior beliefs and attitude toward behavior*—"We found some people think using your [insert specific product here] takes too much time to complete. This might lead to users developing negative attitudes toward our design and prevent some users from wanting to try our product. We want to encourage the belief that use of our product reduces the time it takes to complete [task]. We have included a number of features meant to reduce the perception of time it takes to use our product, including [insert features here]. We think this will lead to increased use of our product."
- *Discussing normative beliefs and subjective norms*—"We included features that will allow users to see what others they know are [doing, purchasing, reading, etc.]. This takes advantage of users' desires to engage in behaviors they think others they know and admire find acceptable. This should promote greater use of our product by users who see others are using it."
- *Discussing control beliefs and perceived control*—"Our design is meant to address a number of ideas that come from psychology. We know that people like to do things that give them a sense of control or increase their perceptions of control. We focused on addressing interactions that enhance users' experiences and increase their feelings of having control over using your product. For example, we have added filters to all search results, created a number of alerts users can opt to receive if certain events happen, and allowed people to customize the information shown on their dashboard screen. We expect these features will provide users with a greater sense of control and enhance their use of your — 'product'."

## 2.5    *Case study: Hotels.com*

Hotels.com is a web application that aggregates hotels and presents users with travel discounts and package deals. Let's deconstruct Hotels.com using the concepts of planned behavior.

### 2.5.1    *Hotels.com: behavior beliefs*

Hotels.com addresses the belief that users will save, highlighting potential savings in multiple ways (figure 2.11). The Deal of the Day clearly states the user is receiving a time-limited 25 % discount and displays the higher prices of four competing websites. They're showing users that they're saving money, and they're doing the extra legwork of searching other discount sites on users' behalf.

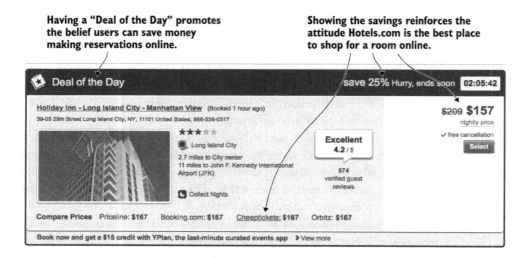

**Figure 2.11   Hotels.com's Deal of the Day fosters positive behavior beliefs about using the product to save money on travel.**

### 2.5.2 *Hotels.com: normative beliefs*

Hotels.com creates and promotes positive normative beliefs about using the site (figure 2.12) by

- Highlighting other users who have recently booked the hotel ("Others just like you have used our site to book this exact property!")
- Showing users the rating and comments from reviews from TripAdvisor users ("Look, we are part of a broad travel network!")
- Showing and allowing Likes via Facebook ("See? Other people like this!")

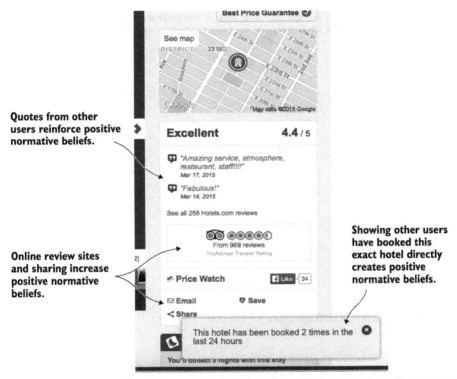

**Figure 2.12 Hotels.com uses social components to enhance the perception that using their product is a social norm.**

### 2.5.3 *Hotels.com: control*

Hotels.com addresses control beliefs in multiple ways (figure 2.13):

- Price Watch ("You can pull the trigger when the price is right; we'll even tell you when!")
- Mobile app ("Book your hotel on the go from any device")
- Package deals ("You know the price of your hotel *and* your flight; no guessing")
- Travel guides ("No need to think about what you can do at your destination")
- Toll-free customer service number ("Can't figure out our site? Call us")

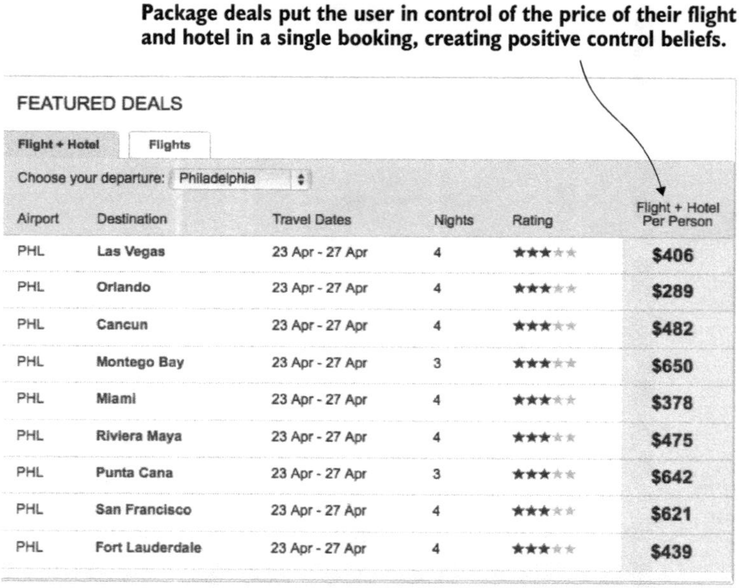

**Package deals put the user in control of the price of their flight and hotel in a single booking, creating positive control beliefs.**

FEATURED DEALS

| Airport | Destination | Travel Dates | Nights | Rating | Flight + Hotel Per Person |
|---------|-------------|--------------|--------|--------|---------------------------|
| PHL | Las Vegas | 23 Apr - 27 Apr | 4 | ★★★☆☆ | $406 |
| PHL | Orlando | 23 Apr - 27 Apr | 4 | ★★★☆☆ | $289 |
| PHL | Cancun | 23 Apr - 27 Apr | 4 | ★★★☆☆ | $482 |
| PHL | Montego Bay | 23 Apr - 27 Apr | 3 | ★★★☆☆ | $650 |
| PHL | Miami | 23 Apr - 27 Apr | 4 | ★★★☆☆ | $378 |
| PHL | Riviera Maya | 23 Apr - 27 Apr | 4 | ★★★☆☆ | $475 |
| PHL | Punta Cana | 23 Apr - 27 Apr | 3 | ★★★☆☆ | $642 |
| PHL | San Francisco | 23 Apr - 27 Apr | 4 | ★★★☆☆ | $621 |
| PHL | Fort Lauderdale | 23 Apr - 27 Apr | 4 | ★★★☆☆ | $439 |

**Figure 2.13   Hotels.com package deals put the user in control.**

## 2.6 *End-of-chapter exercise: applying planned behavior research to design*

Now that you've learned about the psychological principle of planned behavior, let's practice creating design recommendations based on the different components that make up this principle. I've provided a scenario and interview responses from fictitious potential users. Please read through the scenario and the responses and then answer the questions at the end. You can share your answers and provide feedback on the Manning Publications forum here: https://forums.manning.com/forums/design-for-the-mind.

### 2.6.1 Scenario

You are a lead member of a design team creating a website and mobile application that matches people looking for pets to people looking to place (sell and adopt) pets. The site includes dogs, cats, fish, and other common household pets—not exotic animals or ones that come from puppy mills. Users looking to purchase or adopt a pet complete a detailed assessment to determine which pet or pets would be best for them. The site then matches with people looking to sell or adopt out pets based on the criteria of the pets these people have entered.

Working with your UX researcher, your team created an interview protocol to focus on potential pet finders (users) meant to answer the following questions:

1 What are users' behavioral beliefs toward using digital channels to acquire a pet?
2 What are users' normative beliefs toward using digital channels to acquire a pet?
3 What control factors exist for users to acquire a pet using digital channels?

### 2.6.2 Participants

Your team recruits three potential users to complete the interview:
**Participant 1:** A 33-year-old single parent working two jobs
**Participant 2:** A 12-year-old who loves animals
**Participant 3:** A 65-year-old who believes in rescuing pets

### 2.6.3 Data

Your researcher conducts the interviews and collects the following data from the three participants:

**WHAT ARE USERS' BEHAVIORAL BELIEFS TOWARD USING DIGITAL CHANNELS TO ACQUIRE A PET?**
What do you see as the advantages of using a website or mobile application to acquire a pet?

- **Participant 1:** I think the biggest advantage is that I can do it from home. I don't have to go out with my kids to look at a pet until we find one we think we like. Also, knowing how much they will cost ahead of time would be important. I don't want to be surprised by the cost.
- **Participant 2:** I get to see lots of different pets at the same time. I love every kind of animal. I can look at puppies and fish on the same page.
- **Participant 3:** It would only be useful if it told me what pets are up for adoption or rescue. Then I would want to see which ones are in shelters that might euthanize them, and when this would happen. I'd want to rescue the ones closest to death to find them homes.

What do you see as the disadvantages of using a website or mobile application to acquire a pet?

- **Participant 1:** The biggest disadvantage would be that my kids would spend their time looking at pets and pestering me to get one. Ha, ha! They are always begging me for a pet.

- **Participant 2:** How would you even know where these pets are? How would you get them? What if someone else got the one you wanted while you were asking your parents?
- **Participant 3:** That the pigs running puppy mills would be making even more money and creating even more demand for their product.

#### WHERE DO USERS' NORMATIVE BELIEFS TOWARD USING DIGITAL CHANNELS TO ACQUIRE A PET COME FROM?

Please list the individuals or groups who would approve or think you should use a website or mobile application to acquire a pet:

- **Participant 1:** My kids and their friends, the people listing pets on the site
- **Participant 2:** My friends, my uncle who loves animals, people who use Petfinder, people who look for dogs and stuff online on other websites
- **Participant 3:** Overpopulated animal shelters if they can list on the site; pet breeders; veterinarians because it would increase business

Please list the individuals or groups who would disapprove or think you shouldn't use a website or mobile application to acquire a pet.

- **Participant 1:** My mother, the kids' grandmother; she would not think it is a good idea to bring home a pet without the kids meeting it in person. Also, people selling pets on other sites like Craigslist.
- **Participant 2:** My friend's dad is a dog breeder. He would want people to buy dogs from him.
- **Participant 3:** My friends and the other volunteers at the animal shelter. I think my vet would disapprove. Sarah McLachlan.

#### WHAT POTENTIAL CONTROL FACTORS EXIST FOR USING DIGITAL CHANNELS TO ACQUIRE A PET?

Please list any factors or circumstances that would make it easy or enable you to use a website or mobile application to acquire a pet.

- **Participant 1:** Being able to look at what's available in my free time, like on a break at work. Sending pictures and links of the animals I see to my kids. Being able to read descriptions about how the pet is around children and what other important traits it has.
- **Participant 2:** I have an iPad and a smartphone. My parents let me use their laptop sometimes.
- **Participant 3:** Everyone can get online to see things. Even if you don't have a computer, you can do it at the library. That's my worry; you're making it too easy to find a pet. You should be making it harder for people to get a pet, unless it is a rescue.

Please list any factors or circumstances that would make it difficult or prevent you from using a website or mobile application to acquire a pet.

- **Participant 1:** Time. I rarely have it. I would need to have time to sit down and really make a decision. I imagine something like this could take hours of looking at pets until you find one that's perfect. Also, financially it is costly to have a pet. Even a free dog isn't free!

- **Participant 2:** I would need my parents' permission. I don't have any money or a job to raise money. I already have two dogs and a cat, so that is a lot of animals.
- **Participant 3:** I couldn't shop for a pet unless it was a rescue. I don't usually purchase things online.

### 2.6.4 Questions

Thinking about the data the three participants provided, please answer the following questions:

- What are three design recommendations meant to address behavioral beliefs you would make based on the data?
- What are two recommendations you would make for content communicating to potential users how your product addresses their behavioral beliefs?
- What are three design recommendations meant to address normative beliefs you would make based on the data?
- What are two recommendations you would make for content communicating to potential users how your product addresses their normative beliefs?
- What are three design recommendations meant to address control beliefs you would make based on the data?
- What are two recommendations you would make for content communicating to potential users how your product addresses their control beliefs?
- Which of your design recommendations would have the biggest impact? Why?
- Do you think you can address each participant's needs with your design?
- How would you prioritize addressing the participants' concerns?
- What additional data could you collect to inform your design?
- What other user types might exist who are not accounted for? How would you account for them if you did not have resources to conduct additional research?

## 2.7 Additional resources

Ajzen, I. (1991). The theory of planned behavior. *Organizational behavior and human decision processes*, 50(2), 179-211. (One of Ajzen's original articles describing the components of planned behavior.)

——————. (2002). Constructing a TPB questionnaire: Conceptual and methodological considerations. (Ajzen explains how to create questions to gain information from potential users on planned behavior.) See http://mng.bz/RCdA.

——————. (2011). The theory of planned behavior: Reactions and reflections. *Psychology & Health*, 26(9), 1113–1127. (A more recent update from Ajzen on planned behavior.)

George, J. F. (2004). The theory of planned behavior and internet purchasing. *Internet Research*, 14(3), 198–212. (A paper on the application of planned behavior to e-commerce.)

Hansen, T., J.M. Jensen, and H.S. Solgaard. (2004). Predicting online grocery buying intention: A comparison of the theory of reasoned action and the theory of planned behavior. *International Journal of Information Management*, 24(6), 539–550. (A study comparing the Theory of Planned Behavior and the Theory of Reasoned Action in predicting online behavior.)

Hrubes, D., I. Ajzen, and J. Daigle. (2001). Predicting hunting intentions and behavior: An application of the theory of planned behavior. *Leisure Sciences*, 23(3), 165–178. (One of Ajzen's studies examining hunting.)

Pelling, E. L. and K.M. White (2009). The theory of planned behavior applied to young people's use of social networking websites. *CyberPsychology & Behavior*, 12(6), 755–759. (A study on the application of planned behavior to use of social networking sites.)

KEYWORDS: behavioral beliefs, theory of planned behavior, theory of reasoned action, behavioral intention

## 2.8    *Summary*

- You can use the information in this chapter to proactively shape your design to address users' planned behaviors (those they think about before engaging in).
- Planned behavior consists of users' beliefs around behavior, social norms, and control.
- Behavior beliefs are those a user holds toward the outcome of the behavior you're trying to promote (is the result of the behavior positive, negative, or neutral?).
- Social norm beliefs are how your users view the social acceptability others hold toward a behavior.
- Control beliefs are whether users believe they have control over engaging in a behavior.
- You design to address behavior beliefs when you ensure your product is usable and leads to a positive outcome, such as saving money, reducing effort, or saving time.
- You design to address normative beliefs when you show users that others they know or admire use your product, that your product is socially acceptable, and that your product facilitates sharing or social interactions.
- You design to address control beliefs when you empower users with the ability to easily access and control information, such as filters and sorting, surfacing information from multiple sources, and allowing users a variety of settings.
- Addressing one or more of the components of planned behavior increases the likelihood a user will use your product.
- Understanding your users is key to successfully designing for planned behavior and incorporating a number of design elements to address a range of potential user preferences.

# Risky decisions and mental shortcuts

Ernie just got paid and wants to earn extra money. He thinks about all the things he could do that might turn his paycheck into more money: buy lottery tickets, gamble online, gamble on horse racing, invest in stocks …. Ernie quickly rules out buying lottery tickets and investing in stocks based on personal preferences. Next, he evaluates his remaining choices. He ends up choosing gambling online because he thinks the odds are in his favor if he plays correctly. Specifically, Ernie thinks gambling on FullTilt.com is a good way to increase his money. He has seen commercials claiming that FullTilt has the best odds, and it's the first gaming site that comes to his mind.

Ernie logs into his account on FullTilt.com to play poker. He has $50 left over from paying his bills and he wants to see if he can turn it into a bit extra. Ernie decides if he loses $10, he'll quit the game for the day. Ernie begins gambling with the lowest amount he can to enter the game. Ernie immediately wins the first two rounds he plays and then cashes out with $55—a gain of $5.

Life is full of situations with uncertain outcomes. For example, you have a 75% chance of making the train on time if you leave home right now—should you leave now or wait for the next train? Or, you can buy your dream house right now, but if you wait one month, there's a 49% chance it might go down in price and a 51% chance it'll increase in price. What should you do? We refer to these decisions as *risky* because the outcome isn't guaranteed.

Oftentimes, people use mental shortcuts called *heuristics* to reduce the effort of making a decision, especially when outcomes are uncertain or time is constrained. You might not have the time or want to invest in the effort of determining if you'll make the train on time each day. That's where you use heuristics. Assuming you made yesterday's train, the familiarity heuristic will tell you if you leave at the same time today as you did yesterday, you'll make the train. The familiarity heuristic, one of many heuristics researchers have identified, states that people tend to assume the outcomes of decisions from the past will hold true in the future.

Chapter 2 focused on principles for identifying what leads to planned behavior. Your design also needs to account for how individuals respond to decisions in which the outcome is less clear or they have less time to decide (figure 3.1). Risk analysis, management, and communication is a field of study that examines how people analyze risk and make decisions under uncertainty. You're familiar with many of these situations: playing

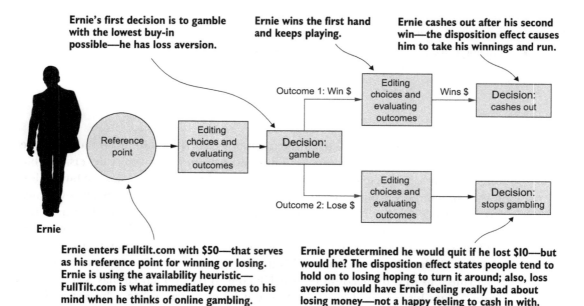

**Figure 3.1   The disposition effect, loss aversion, and reference point are all part of making decisions under risk and uncertainty. Heuristics, such as the availability heuristic, are mental shortcuts people use to make decisions.**

the lottery, skydiving, bidding for an item on eBay, or choosing to use one website over another to purchase a new pair of shoes. This chapter focuses on how design can influence these types of decisions. For example, you'll know why it's important to place key features, such as the account login, in places users are familiar with looking for them.

> **NOTE** You can create a powerful experience that accounts for both planned behavior and the mental shortcuts people take by combining knowledge of how people make decisions involving risk with the principle of planned behavior covered in the previous chapter.

## 3.1 Introduction

Individuals assign different values to decisions based on the possibility of the outcome leading to a gain or a loss. More important, individuals don't weigh outcomes solely on their face value. A $50 gain isn't viewed with the same value as a $50 loss—people use mental shortcuts and aren't as logical as economics researchers assumed.

### 3.1.1 Academic background

Daniel Kahneman and Amos Tversky, highly regarded academics in the field of economics, published a groundbreaking article (see the additional resources) exploring much of what I'll cover in this chapter. They were interested in understanding how people make decisions when they're in situations with uncertain outcomes. At the time, academics thought most people made decisions to maximize their financial gain. Kahneman and Tversky didn't see things the same way. They thought people considered a number of other factors in determining their decisions, such as brand loyalty, certainty of a gain or loss, and what had happened the last time they made a similar decision.

The researchers set up a number of studies starting in the 1970s to determine how people make decisions. They'd ask people to choose from various options that led to outcomes viewed as a loss or a gain. The outcome of these studies showed that people don't behave in an economically rational sense; they're notoriously risk-averse, and they want a guaranteed positive outcome. Also, people spend too much time worrying about the likelihood of bad, yet less likely, things occurring. For example, in one study researchers offered people a guaranteed amount of money or a 50% chance of getting an amount of money that was much more than the guaranteed amount. Most people picked the guaranteed amount of money. Another study found that people were more likely to overestimate the likelihood of dying from an unnatural cause such as an accident or homicide than a more likely natural cause such as heart disease. When the researchers reported their findings, it was the definition of an aha! moment for the field of behavioral economics.

Out of Kahneman and Tversky's research came a new idea called *prospect theory*, which has been well received. Kahneman received a Nobel Prize in economics based in part on this work. Economists now use many of the ideas from prospect theory to explain everyday human behavior. For example, the larger a lottery jackpot becomes, the greater the number of people who buy tickets, even though the odds of winning don't change. Another interesting example of research using concepts from prospect theory involves the price of orange juice. People are more likely to switch brands of orange juice if they think they're saving money on a product they perceive as higher quality than what they currently drink. People aren't likely to switch brands just to save money on a product they perceive as lower quality than their reference point. In other words, even if you have a sale, people won't switch to your product if they perceive it as lower quality than what they currently use.

Essentially, researchers have found that rather than making rational decisions and giving each potential outcome equal weight, people attach emotion, mental heuristics, and perceptions to their decisions. We need to understand outside factors related to emotion, heuristics, and perceptions if we want to understand why and how people make decisions.

### AN EXAMPLE

People use emotions and heuristics to make big and small decisions. Arthur is in the market for a new house. He views a number of houses and then narrows down his choices to two two-bedroom houses he can afford (although he feels emotional eliminating some of the houses he really liked). He then evaluates his remaining two choices. For house 1, Arthur hates the electric-blue paint on the bedroom walls. He's a terrible painter and the last time he tried to paint a house it led to a huge waste of his time (and a mess). The familiarity heuristic leads Arthur to believe he'll suffer the same outcome if he needs to repaint his new house. House 2 is being sold as is and has a roof in questionable condition. Arthur realizes he'll need to spend thousands of additional dollars to repair the roof shortly after he moves in. Loss aversion causes Arthur not to put a bid on this house.

Both houses represented risky decisions: house 1 might lead to a painting catastrophe, and house 2 might lead to a lot of extra expense soon after moving in. Loss aversion wins out over the familiarity heuristic, and Arthur places the winning bid on the first house.

Arthur still needs to deal with the issue of painting the house. Days after Arthur moves into his new house, he logs on to Handy.com (figure 3.2) and hires a painter to repaint his bedrooms. The certainty effect (section 3.2.3) causes Arthur to feel relief in the decision to hire a professional painter who will get the job done. The 100% money-back guarantee serves as an insurance policy or warranty to Arthur as well.

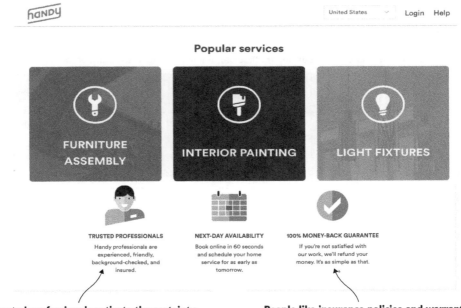

Figure 3.2 Handy's product appeals to the decision-making process of individuals not wanting to risk doing their own home repairs.

## 3.2 *Key concepts of decision-making under risk*

According to principles of decision-making under risk, people go through two defined stages during this process: *editing* and *evaluation*. In the editing stage, people take all the outcomes they're aware of, rank them in the order from best to worst (based on a whole lot more than dollar value), forget about the worst, and choose the best to keep in consideration. In the evaluation stage, people look at the best remaining options, attach the subjective weight to these outcomes, and make their decision.

Let's take a closer look at the stages so we can learn how to support our users as they go through them.

### 3.2.1 *First, people go through editing*

Individuals begin editing when faced with making a decision involving an uncertain outcome. When individuals enter editing mode, they first must have a starting point to determine if an outcome will leave them better or worse off. They then determine if an outcome is positive or negative, which outcomes cancel each other out, and which outcomes are clearly inferior or dominant (and therefore don't need further consideration).

For example, Azuka might have an opportunity to buy a raffle ticket for $20. The ticket has a .00001% chance of winning $1 million. First, she'll look at her current state. Let's say Azuka has $40 in cash in her pocket. She'll use that as her baseline. She then considers the three options in table 3.1.

Table 3.1   Azuka's three options for purchasing a raffle ticket. Although this table makes Azuka's process look well thought out and methodical, it's happening in the blink of an eye.

| | Number of raffle tickets | Cost | Potential positive outcome | Potential negative outcome |
|---|---|---|---|---|
| Option 1 | None | $0 | Save $40 to spend on other items | Will have no chance to win the raffle |
| Option 2 | One | $20 | Will win $1 million | Will lose the $20 she paid for the ticket |
| Option 3 | Two | $40 | Will win $1 million | Will lose the $40 she paid for the tickets |

Azuka will (quickly and most likely unconsciously) order these decisions and cancel the unacceptable ones. She finds Option 3 unacceptable—she'll need at least $20 to make other purchases. This leaves two options: pay $20 for one raffle ticket with .00001% of winning $1 million or don't buy the ticket.

Azuka now moves into the evaluation stage of decision-making.

### 3.2.2   *Next, people go through evaluation*

Individuals examine all of the outcomes still under consideration after the editing stage and select the one with the highest value in the evaluation stage. Again, this happens very quickly. Part of this process involves attaching a weight to the probability of each decision. This is different from logical and objective decision-making in that the weight can be subjective, based on whether the outcome is a gain or a loss, and which heuristic an individual uses to order the choices. Heuristics, the mental shortcuts I mentioned earlier, play a critical role in how people will assign a weight to a decision.

Keep in mind that a gain or loss doesn't have to be strictly financial. A gain or loss in time, productivity, or other limited resource can also determine the outcome of an evaluation. You might be trying to decide whether to fly or drive to a vacation destination, for example. Your decision to drive might save money on the surface, but you'll need to factor in the amount of time you'll spend getting to your destination, and what value you place on that time, before deciding which is a greater gain or loss.

Individuals will then engage in the behavior (place the bet, buy a product) after they complete their evaluation. Users might also choose not to engage in any behavior if they determine that engaging in the behavior (using your product) is a loss versus not doing anything. Some users might delay the decision if they're unclear as to the risk; this is where your design decisions are critical—if you successfully incorporate psychology into your design, you're more likely to experience success with these potential users.

Azuka evaluates her remaining options of purchasing one raffle ticket or none. Loss aversion tells her she really doesn't want to throw her money away on nothing. She can't think of a single person she knows who has won the raffle in the past (availability heuristic), and the last time she bought a raffle ticket she lost (familiarity heuristic). Azuka decides to purchase gas with her money she'd have spent on the raffle ticket. As she checks out at the gas station, she sees a key ring with a kitten on it. Kittens make Azuka so happy! She immediately, and without regret, purchases the key ring (affect heuristic)!

### 3.2.3 *What impacts the evaluation of uncertain decisions*

People make decisions that lead to behavior: they decide either to do something or not do it. Outcomes are attached to each behavior, and people attach a positive or negative outcome to the decision made. If someone uses your website to purchase shoes and the wrong pair is shipped, that person will assign a negative outcome to use of your website. People assign different values to the potential outcomes that exist for a decision. Individuals consider a number of possibilities when assigning weight, starting with whether they view the outcome as a gain or loss—more often, they view negative outcomes stronger than positive outcomes.

This section will cover a number of key factors affecting the decisions people make:

- Reference point
- Loss aversion
- Certainty effect
- Disposition effect
- Purchase of insurance and warranties

#### REFERENCE POINT AND LOSS AVERSION

People enter a decision-making scenario with a reference point. Individuals view a potential outcome as a gain or a loss based on this reference point. If I have $40, that might be my reference point. I'd consider any decision leading to greater than $40 a gain.

Researchers have found that people assign a greater value to losses than to gains (figure 3.3). Individuals experience more pain with a loss than the amount of joy when they experience an equal gain. I'd feel fairly happy if I found $10 and now had $50 in cash. But I'd feel much more unhappiness if I lost $10 and was down to $30 in cash. This leads people to engage in loss-averse behaviors—they want to avoid feeling loss. This has a major effect on decision-making.

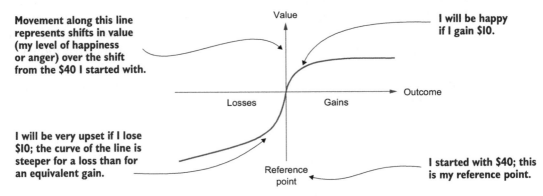

**Figure 3.3** A visual depiction that people experience greater pain from a loss than the joy they experience over an equivalent gain

## CERTAINTY EFFECT

How would you answer the two following problems?

- Problem 1: Which of the following would you choose?
  - 50% chance to win a three-week tour of England, France, and Italy
  - A one-week tour of England with certainty

- Problem 2: Which of the following would you choose?
  - 5% chance to win a three-week tour of England, France, and Italy
  - 10% chance to win a one-week tour of England

Researchers found the results for problem 1 showed that 78% of participants selected option B. The results for problem 2 showed that 67% of participants selected option A. The researchers concluded that people prefer outcomes that are guaranteed over outcomes only considered possible (option B in problem 1 is guaranteed, whereas option A is only possible). But when no outcome is guaranteed, people become more likely to choose the option that has the largest gain (or lowest loss), even if it involves more risk (option A in problem 2 offers a larger potential win, whereas option B has a higher chance of winning).

The researchers labeled this the *certainty effect*. People are more likely to make a decision that leads to a sure (certain) gain. When all outcomes are uncertain, people are more likely to engage in riskier decisions with better potential outcomes.

## THE DISPOSITION EFFECT

People cash in on a guaranteed gain too quickly and hold on for the potential to turn around a loss for too long. Researchers frequently observe this behavior in financial trading. Investors sell winners too soon; they offload stock that has gained value before the stock reaches its peak price. Investors hold on to bad stock too long on the hope that it will turn around and earn back the value lost, often leading to a greater loss. The disposition effect explains the double-or-nothing concept. Once individuals have experienced a loss, they're willing to engage in riskier behavior to make up the loss.

## PURCHASE OF INSURANCE AND WARRANTIES

People overweigh the probability of suffering a loss. Researchers tell us that this explains why (aside from being legally mandated) people purchase insurance for things like automobile crashes, home fires, theft, and other low-probability events. Researchers point out that people are willing to take concrete action (pay money on a premium) for an unlikely event (statistically, most people don't experience catastrophic events). The thought of experiencing a loss is worth the behavior of proactively paying to help avoid the loss.

Warranties serve as another example of this practice. Best Buy attempts to sell its Geek Squad Protection (figure 3.4) plan to customers purchasing a large appliance or electronic device. The people purchasing these warranties are seeking peace of mind in the unlikely event their purchase suffers a major failure after the included manufacturer's warranty expires.

**Figure 3.4   Extended warranties: making coffee spills on your computer like they never happened**

## 3.3   *How to design for decisions under risk*

Your design can incorporate much of what we know about how people make decisions under risk. Researchers have identified key psychological concepts that are inherent to decisions people make while shopping, while considering how to donate their time, and so forth. Let's look at some examples of how you can apply this information to your work.

### 3.3.1   *Determine users' reference point*

The first task you need to engage in is to determine what reference point users set for your product. You want users to experience a gain in relation to the reference point they're setting. Users' reference points directly relate to the type of product you offer. Here are three examples:

- Financial products are expected to make users money, making the amount of cash at the start of using your product the reference point. Users gaining money will experience positive feelings toward your product. If users lose money, they'll experience negative feelings.

- Organizational products are expected to save users time and keep their lives in order. The reference point is the current amount of time they're spending on organization and the level of order they feel in their lives. If users feel like they're taking more time or they're less organized after using your product, they'll consider this a loss. If users believe they're saving time and they're more organized, they'll view this as a gain.

- Social media products are expected to connect users with relevant people, products, and information. The reference point will be the number of and relevancy of connections users expect when they join, and the ease with which they connect to additional peers. If users increase their connections, this will be considered a gain. If users experience fewer connections, or are frustrated with irrelevant connections, they'll consider this a loss.

Travel search engine Kayak (figure 3.5) provides users with a reference point when they present the results of a search. Kayak's algorithm comes up with a suggestion of "buy now" or "wait" based on past price fluctuations. Kayak then allows users to create an alert that will tell them if prices have strayed from this reference point.

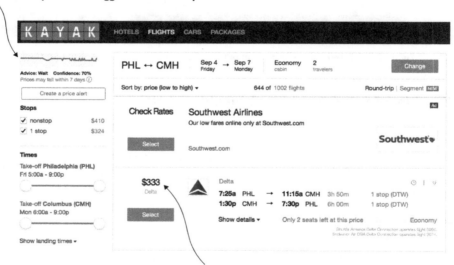

Figure 3.5  Kayak provides users with a reference point to assist them in making their decision to purchase a plane ticket.

**HOW TO DESIGN FOR YOUR USERS' REFERENCE POINT**

You need to understand what reference point your users have and how they set this reference point in order to accommodate them in your design. I recommend

- Conducting interviews to understand users' process of setting a reference point
- Developing a series of questions to uncover the purpose users give your product and what they'd determine as a gain or a loss when using your product
- Administering surveys to determine common reference points for your product

You might find more than one reference point. You can use this information to strengthen your design and address the features contributing to the reference point. You can also use this information to help guide your education and marketing efforts. Your user registration process provides an opportunity to shift users' reference point. Let's say you find that users would consider additional time spent setting up individualized preferences as a loss. You can guide users through setting preferences in your onboarding or registration process and they won't have to think about it in the future unless they choose to.

Other ways for your design to show users how they've saved time or money based on their initial reference point are the following:

- Provide inline error messages and field validation when users enter data; this saves time compared to redoing a form after it has been submitted incorrectly.
- Show users what they're saving compared to a previous price.
- Show users how much time they've saved by using your product.
- Show users the accuracy rate of your product in accomplishing a task.
- Show users whether a price has increased or decreased since the last time they viewed or purchased an item.

### 3.3.2 *Define and design for users' decision points*

You need to understand where people are making decisions and create a design that makes them feel more empowered toward making the decision. Define what decisions you're asking people to make, and the frequency with which decisions occur in the use of your design. Is use of your product an occasional thing, or will people be logging in to update something daily? Your answer impacts how often users have to make a decision.

Users often need assistance with making decisions. Your design should facilitate easy decision-making. ALEX (figure 3.6) is a product meant to assist users in making decisions about healthcare and other employee benefits. ALEX asks users a number of questions and then makes recommendations in everyday language, reducing the mental burden of choosing the right benefits. How can you make your product more like ALEX? What can you do to facilitate easy decision-making on your site or application?

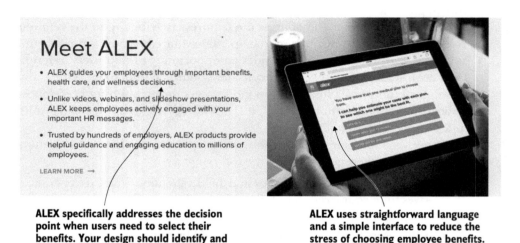

**ALEX specifically addresses the decision point when users need to select their benefits. Your design should identify and address users' key decision points.**

**ALEX uses straightforward language and a simple interface to reduce the stress of choosing employee benefits.**

**Figure 3.6   ALEX exemplifies a product designed to assist with decision points. How can you make your design like ALEX?**

### HOW TO DESIGN FOR USERS' DECISION POINTS

The first decision all users must make is whether or not to use your product to accomplish the task they wish to complete. Additional decision points you need to design for include the following:

- When are users determining potential outcomes of using your product?
- What potential positive and negative outcomes will users imagine?
- When do users expect to engage with your product?
- Where do users expect to engage with your product?
- What type of device will your users want to use?
- When do you present users with options to make a purchase or upgrade?
- Can you provide recommendations to users at specific decision points?

You need to respect users' time when it comes to making decisions. If your product requires users to first set up a profile, you might wait before asking them to immediately make a payment. This avoids users' loss of money and time simultaneously. You can consider allowing users time to experience your product after setting up their profile so they feel a gain in productivity, and then present them with payment options. Perhaps this comes in the form of a free trial or a limited-functionality free version of your product. You should make it clear to users that functionality is limited or, when a trial expires, you don't want to frustrate them if they invest time without realizing they'll need to pay for full access in the future.

### 3.3.3 Design for loss aversion

People experience loss when they feel like they have less of something than what they started with. Loss is not just financial: time, effort, and other resources can be lost. You can use loss aversion as a blueprint for good design. You address loss aversion when you make sure your design is usable and convenient. You can't altogether avoid loss; you want users to spend time on your site completing a profile, searching for goods, or selecting a product. Be strategic about how you introduce losses to your users, and follow up with perceptions of a gain or multiple gains since they'll feel the pain from a loss stronger than a gain. You might ask people to complete a profile (loss of time) so that they can receive customized recommendations (gain back time in the long run) and save their billing information for reuse (gain back time in the long run), and gain access to additional information on your site (gain in resources/knowledge).

You can use loss aversion to increase use of your product. You do this in a number of ways. You can show users they have something now but will lose it if they don't act. If you can show users they'll have access to something specific (gain) but only have a limited time to act (potential loss), for example, they're more likely to engage in the behavior you'd like them to in order to maintain the gain. Ticketmaster (figure 3.7) and StubHub do this by displaying timers while users are purchasing tickets to an event.

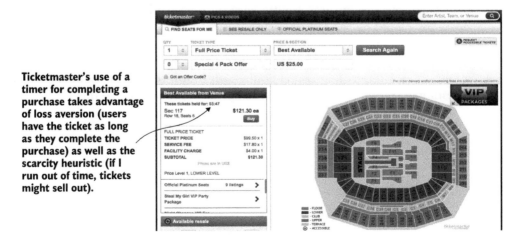

Ticketmaster's use of a timer for completing a purchase takes advantage of loss aversion (users have the ticket as long as they complete the purchase) as well as the scarcity heuristic (if I run out of time, tickets might sell out).

**Figure 3.7 Less than four minutes to buy my ticket to see One Direction. Don't think about it, buy now!**

Your strategy should consider breaking up a big gain into multiple smaller gains, particularly if you also introduce users to a loss (for example, asking them to pay for something). This allows individuals to experience the feeling of a gain more frequently, potentially compensating for the infrequent, yet stronger, feeling of a loss. For instance, rather than offering a free upgrade to use for one month, consider offering four free one-week upgrades for various projects over the course of a year.

You help users avoid loss by making information easy to find when you

- Create navigation categories and subcategories in line with users' expectations (you can access this through a card sort research activity)
- Design your search so that it searches your entire product for what users enter
- Create FAQ categories based on users' mental models (you can also access this through a card sort research activity)
- Use jargon-free terminology for your field labels and links

Your goal is to reduce the amount of loss a user experiences in time and effort, or financially. You should explicitly show how your product reduces loss compared to use of a competitor's (design your product this way). Your design should also allow people to feel like they are making some gains from using your product. If you follow these steps, you'll tap into your users' loss aversion.

### 3.3.4   *Design for the certainty effect*

People like certainty. They're more likely to make a decision that leads to a sure gain. Interestingly, researchers find that people make riskier decisions the less certain an outcome becomes. You should be aware of this for your own behaviors. Design projects are full of uncertainty. Are you taking big risks because the outcome is uncertain? Should you be? I can't answer that, but it's worth having the conversation with your team in which you step back to discuss your level of risk tolerance, what risky decisions your team engages in on a regular basis, and what the standard approach to these decisions should be.

Oracle's Solaris product addresses the certainty effect in a straightforward way with its Binary Application Guarantee (figure 3.8). Oracle Solaris guarantees all binary applications will maintain compatibility with future releases. Customers can rest easy investing in training and software with a product guarantee like this.

---

**Oracle Solaris Binary Application Guarantee**

The Oracle Solaris Binary Application Guarantee reflects Oracle's confidence in the compatibility of applications from one release of Oracle Solaris to the next and is designed to make re-qualification a thing of the past.

If a binary application runs on an OS release of Oracle Solaris 2.6 or later, including their initial release and all updates, it will run the latest releases of Oracle Solaris, including their initial releases and all updates, even if the application has not been recompiled for those latest releases.  Binary compatibility between releases of Oracle Solaris helps protect your long-term investment in the development, training and maintenance of your applications.

If an application experiences a compatibility problem when running on your latest supported Oracle Solaris Operating System, support is offered as described below:

> **For Oracle Solaris 10**
> Use the integrated "appcert" utility (see the man page for appcert) to check your application. If no errors are reported but problems running the application remain, a Service Request (SR) should be opened to obtain support.
>
> **For Oracle Solaris 11**
> There is a new tool for Oracle Solaris 11 to check for application compatibility. The Preflight Application Checker tool can be downloaded from: http://www.oracle.com/technetwork/server-storage/solaris11/downloads/index.html The package includes documentation which describes how to check an application for compatibility with Oracle Solaris 11.

---

**Figure 3.8   Oracle's Solaris Binary Application Guarantee addresses the certainty effect.**

You should ask how you can reduce risk and increase certainty for your users. What can you guarantee users from your design or product standpoint? You might want to

- Display security seals and third-party validations
- Provide transaction numbers and receipts via email
- Offer free updates
- Guarantee the price of your product
- Allow users to specify a time frame of commitment
- Allow users to mask data (such as hiding account balances, displaying only the last four digits of critical data)

### 3.3.5   *Design for the disposition effect*

The *disposition effect* states that people tend to jump out of an investment too soon when an opportunity exists for a gain. People also want to hold on to get back to break-even if they've had a loss. We see the disposition effect in many other contexts outside of investments. We often see users who will sign up for a free trial or limited version of a product, but never move ahead with purchasing the full version. They take the immediate win of a free product and cash out before benefiting from the full functionality. We also see users who fail to upgrade products or hardware, the equivalent of holding on to a loser too long. We all know the person who is still suffering from poor performance and lack of compatibility with current apps because they refuse to update their smartphone to one that's been released within the past three years.

SiriusXM satellite radio has designed its online marketing and promotions to address the disposition effect of cashing out early (figure 3.9). People often receive a free three-month trial of the SiriusXM product after purchasing a new or used car. The disposition effect would suggest most people would then let their subscriptions lapse after the "win" of three free months. Sirius begins to promote renewal to users as soon as the free trial starts. They offer users another five additional months at a discounted rate to continue with the subscription. Sirius is hoping that after eight months of free or discounted service, users will be willing to pay full price to stay on as customers (or maybe they offer additional discounts at that time).

**Figure 3.9   Sirius XM offers additional discounts over time to counter the tendency of users to cash out after a free trial.**

### HOW TO DESIGN FOR THE DISPOSITION EFFECT

I interpret the disposition effect to mean it's difficult to get users to change or update what they're currently using—a mental inertia. If they're using something that's working well for them (considered a win), they're unlikely to look for a newer or better alternative in the future (they cash out). Alternatively, if they're using a product that isn't giving them the benefit they need (a loss), they aren't likely to look for a newer or costly alternative (they hold on to the loser).

Microsoft faces a constant battle to get users to upgrade to its newest OS. For some, the current OS provides what they need, and they don't see the point in the hassle and uncertainty of switching systems (cashing in on the winner they currently use). Others have invested money and time learning the OS they use, even if it's inefficient, and they don't want to lose that investment (holding on to a loser).

Your design needs to encourage users to upgrade to the latest version of your product, switch to your product from what they currently use, or add additional products to what they currently use. You can accomplish this by

- Showing users a side-by-side comparison of your product versus others (what does your product do better or faster than others?)
- Offering free upgrades for a limited time if a user has already purchased an older version
- Discounting package deals with other products you offer
- Offering discounted upgrades to users of competing products
- Offering a free limited-time trial of a new product
- Stopping support of older versions
- Allowing users to enroll in a program of regular automatic upgrades, similar to cell phone carriers offering a new iPhone every year

### 3.3.6 *How to design for heuristics*

In psychology, heuristic is a fancy word meaning mental shortcut. Heuristics play a key role during the evaluation stage of many decisions. Users have so many decisions to make there's no way they could think about all of the pros and cons for each one. Their minds would be overloaded and they'd stop functioning.

Anything can potentially be a heuristic. If your favorite color is green, this might be your heuristic for choosing the shirt you wear. If it's green, you wear it. If you need a new shirt, you buy a green one. That's one less task taking up the precious resources of your decision-making ability. The potential problem with this, or any heuristic, is that you aren't accounting for other variables in your decision. If you've selected what you wear based solely on favorite color, you aren't accounting for the weather or for what activities you might be engaging in that day. An oversimplification for sure, but you get the point.

People frequently use heuristics to make decisions; you should use them to your advantage in your design. Let's explore six common heuristics with examples of how to address them in digital design.

#### AVAILABILITY HEURISTIC

People determine the likelihood of something happening based on how quickly they can think of examples. People assign the highest value or likelihood to the outcomes they think of first. You might influence potential users of your product if your product is what immediately comes to mind as an example of what will solve their problem. You can address this heuristic by supplying users with relevant examples of how your product meets a need they have.

TurboTax (figure 3.10) provides an example of the availability heuristic. TurboTax is widely considered the leader in creating a guided tax filing experience in the United States. It has also become synonymous with e-file and other forms of filing taxes digitally and online. People referring to tax-filing software often default to saying "TurboTax" when referring to the concept of tax software in general (such as, "I still need to jump on TurboTax and get my taxes done"). Think about it; what product would you assume someone used if they said to you "I just filed my taxes using that nifty tax-filing software"?

Often TurboTax gets name-dropped when I'm in meetings with clients who want to create an easy experience that guides users to the desired outcome. How can you make your product the TurboTax of your field?

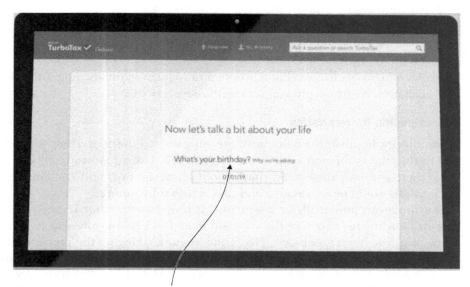

**Clients often reference TurboTax's method of walking users through a workflow as an example of how they want their product to function; TurboTax is their availability heuristic.**

Figure 3.10   TurboTax: setting the standard for self-service experiences

The availability heuristic can also serve to hurt your cause. Let's say you work closely with government agencies and their digital properties. You've likely heard a number of references to the Healthcare.gov debacle during the months following the launch of that product. Healthcare.gov served as the immediate example that came into many people's minds when they thought of government websites. This led to the widespread opinion that government sites are unusable and poorly designed, thanks to a steady barrage of negative news related to healthcare.gov.

You can effectively utilize the availability heuristic when you

- Compare your digital product to a familiar physical product (for example, "Using our personal financial management app is like having your own financial adviser!")
- Make it clear to your users how you want them to use your product

- Include examples or testimonials strategically placed for users
- Remind users of past behavior you want them to engage in repeatedly or searches they've previously engaged in

### EMOTIONAL HEURISTIC

I'm sure I don't need to tell you, but emotions have an effect on decision-making. I don't think it's possible to oversell the importance of emotion in decision-making. Researchers think emotion happens just before thoughts, meaning the emotional tone you set will precede the thoughts that follow. You have to keep this in mind for any product you create.

HooplaHa (figure 3.11) understands the importance of matching the emotion of your site with the message you want to convey. Its mission is simple: to make people smile more. Of course, it highlights puppy dogs on one of the homepage articles. Beyond that, HooplaHa named the navigation categories using happy-sounding terminology: Life, Inspiration, Wellness, and Health.

You need to account for the emotions that facilitate and surround use of your product. Let's say you're designing a website for the purchase of customized gravestones. You wouldn't want to make the visual tone of the site obnoxiously happy.

Make sure your site is compatible with all browsers. Your experience reflects your knowledge and respect for users and their situations. If you provide them with a thoughtless experience, they'll assume you don't respect them.

**Figure 3.11   HooplaHa—I get happy just saying the name.**

You design for addressing emotions when you

- Conduct user interviews and surveys to determine the mood users need for your product to be relevant.
- Conduct usability testing to identify areas in which your product frustrates users.
- Account for positive emotions. If people experience great joy using your product, you're more likely to get them to engage with and use your product.
- Identify opportunities to set that mood through interaction patterns and visual design.
- Incorporate unobtrusive background videos and other media to set the tone (as appropriate).
- Keep in mind that no one wants to feel ambivalent when using your product.

### FAMILIARITY HEURISTIC

Individuals tend to form beliefs and judgments and make decisions on the assumption that what has happened in the past will hold true in the present. This can serve either as a source of safety if past behavior has led to successful decisions or as a source of hazard if previous behavior has led to unsafe situations. A real-life example is that people tend to form relationships that are familiar with the ones they've experienced in the past. If you grow up in a situation where abusive relationships are the norm, that's the type of relationship likely to come to mind when you think of what a relationship looks like.

The familiarity heuristic applies to where you locate important features on your product's design. Close your eyes and tell me where you'd go to log in or out of an account on a webpage. Did you say upper-right corner? I sure did. If people are used to looking at the top of the screen for their sign-on information on the desktop version of Facebook, LinkedIn, and Twitter (figure 3.12), they're probably going to expect to see alerts in the same area on your desktop product (assuming they're frequent users of these products).

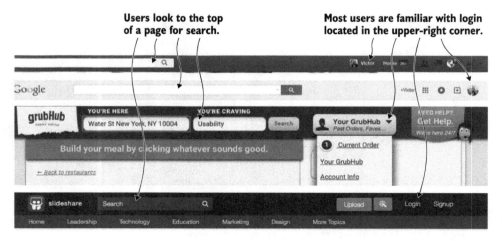

**Figure 3.12   From Facebook to SlideShare, and everything in between, we're used to seeing our account sign-on information in the upper-right corner of the screen.**

You can take advantage of the familiarity heuristic by not trying to reinvent the wheel for design in your field. Users have grown to expect things to look a certain way or be in a certain place. You'll need to meet the expectations your users have. You'll also need to be consistent in your design throughout your product and across platforms. You should do the following:

- Engage in usability testing to validate placement of key features in your product's design.
- Compare your design to your competitors'; identify similarities and differences in features, functionality, and location of page elements such as navigation, search function, filters, and calls to action.
- Create UI design pattern libraries for consistent application of design patterns across your products.
- Be sure your product is functioning correctly and solving the problem that it's supposed to solve.
- Make sure your product works and is bug free *before* launching.

The familiarity heuristic suggests that once users have a negative impression of your product, they'll carry this with them as what they expect next time they consider using your product. You already knew it was important to make a good first impression; now you know one way to describe why.

### ESCALATION OF COMMITMENT HEURISTIC

No one likes wasting time. The escalation of commitment heuristic speaks to this fact. Also known as the sunken cost commitment, this heuristic leads to individuals remaining committed to an action or decision based on the prior investment of time they've made.

IT projects that go over time and budget serve as an example of escalation of commitment. According to the folks at McKinsey & Company (see the additional resources), IT projects go over budget 45% of the time and over the period allotted 7% of the time, with software projects having the greatest overage. Yet most of these projects are seen to completion. People tend to look at the investment of time they've made in something as a reflection of the need for future commitment. In other words, people hate to think all the time they've spent nurturing a relationship or developing a project will have been for naught if the relationship or project ends. This can be true, even if from this day forth they'll derive no more joy or utility from the relationship that they benefited from in the past, or if the project becomes obsolete before it's completed.

The escalation of commitment suggests the more time people feel like they've spent building a relationship with your product, or the greater financial commitment they make, the less likely they'll be to stray to a competitor's product. This doesn't mean you can relax once you've gotten users to invest time or money in your product. This means you do need to focus on smart ways of having users invest time, money, or effort in your product in the beginning if you want them to stay users. Your competition will stand a better chance of luring your customers away if users don't feel there's any penalty in time or money for switching. You should address the escalation of commitment in your product's onboarding process.

You want users to invest time and resources in your product, and you want them to feel worthwhile doing so. You can consider incentivizing longevity the way insurance companies often do, providing accident forgiveness every two years as a customer. Cell phone companies reward longevity as well, providing a discount on an upgrade after a customer spends a specified amount of time under a contract. You can entice users to spend more time on your product in many ways, leading to a stronger bond between users and your product.

Banking clients I've worked with seem especially aware of this critical heuristic. They've done a good job identifying "sticky behaviors": signing up for direct deposit, enrolling in online bill pay, setting up online banking, and so forth. The more of these sticky behaviors users engage in within the first 90 days as a client, the more likely this user will still be a client a year later.

You need to identify the sticky behaviors associated with your product. Users engaging in these behaviors are the ones demonstrating a likely future commitment to your product. You then need to highlight these behaviors as part of your onboarding process. If your product had a social aspect, you'd want users to complete their profile, add a picture, and do other tasks that reflect an investment of time.

### SCARCITY HEURISTIC

You can drive people to use your product by creating a perception of scarcity. Users are likely to engage in a behavior that makes them part of an exclusive group. Users are also more likely to purchase an item now versus waiting for later if they know there are limited items of the quantity. Overstock.com (figure 3.13) and many other e-commerce sites inspire the scarcity heuristic when they display the quantity of stock an item has left.

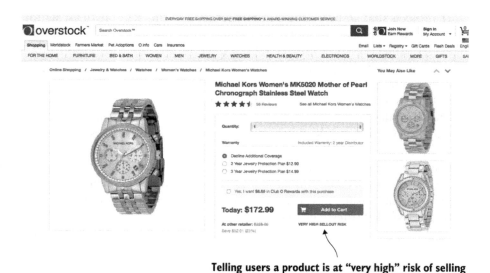

Telling users a product is at "very high" risk of selling out takes advantage of the scarcity heuristic.

**Figure 3.13   Overstock.com provides a strategically located message suggesting product scarcity.**

You should consider some of the following techniques if they're in line with your product:

- Limited edition(s) with exclusive features
- Invitation-only releases
- Pre-sales for loyal customers
- Special events (such as 12-hour sales only on purchases made through your mobile app)

#### STEREOTYPES

Stereotypes are heuristics. Why bother to get to know the teenager hanging out on the street corner—you already know he's up to no good. The tallest kid in class must be good at basketball. You get the point. Stereotypes provide us with a shortcut to judge who we feel we'll be like and who we think is too different for us to associate with. I've already mentioned that heuristics can be faulty, especially if you rely on them.

I'll never recommend incorporating stereotypes into your design. I challenge you to identify the stereotypes you or others on your design team assume, and gather valid data to either back up these assertions or dispel them. You should also engage in research to uncover the stereotypes your users have about your product and users of your product. This will help you understand why some people are attracted to your product.

### 3.4 *Talking the talk: Conversations about decisions under risk and users' mental shortcuts*

Decisions under risk pave the way for us to discuss critical components of our design features and strategy with our clients, peers, and users. People should find elements of this principle easily relatable. Use some of the following discussion points to start the conversation about heuristics with your clients or peers:

- *Discussing loss aversion*—"We know users hate paying fees. Our onboarding process guides users through learning about the account options available, what the costs are, and how they can lower or avoid fees."
- *Discussing escalation of commitment*—"We know users value their time. This applies to the time it takes to become a customer and the time it would take to leave your business for a competitor. Our design accounts for both aspects of valuing time. We've created an express enrollment form to get users up and running in a matter of minutes. Over time, we'll engage users in a series of quick tasks that as a whole reflect a significant investment of time: entering and saving a credit card for future use, attaching the account to their social media feeds, and having users create a detailed profile for other users to view. We know that users engaging in these options will feel invested in your product. These users will view the prospect of leaving for a competitor as a loss in the time they've spent building a deep profile with your —'product'."
- *Discussing the availability heuristic*—"We know prospective users have mental shortcuts they take when deciding to use a product. We've added recommended products to the homepage of your website. We expect this to lead to greater sales of these products based on making them available to users' memories. You'll be

able to alternate what users see when landing on your homepage based on an algorithm that keeps track of which products need a boost in sales, which ones have been selling the hottest over the past 24 hours, and so forth. You'll also be able to insert whatever product you feel needs highlighting."

- *Discussing stereotypes*—"Your site uses pictures of seemingly heterosexual Caucasian families whenever displaying a 'family'-focused product. The term *family* has an ever shifting and diverse meaning to your potential users. Your use of images should reflect this. Potential users will view this as a sign of respect and that your company embraces diversity."

## 3.5    *Case study: eBay*

Auctions are inherently risky for all involved. People selling items run the risk of having a precious item sell for much less than the expected value. People placing bids risk having someone outbid them, or having to increase their bid to an amount greater than they'd anticipated in order to win the auction. eBay has been making money off the principles covered in this chapter faster than an auctioneer can holler off the price of the next bid.

Let's break down the success of the online auction house using what you've learned. You're likely familiar with eBay even if you don't use the site to buy or sell items. The brand has become part of the conversation when people discuss internet business models and success stories. "eBaying" something has become synonymous with making an online sale or purchase, particularly of an obscure or preowned item. You'll also see that many of the affordances of digital experiences allow eBay to succeed well beyond what traditional brick-and-mortar auction houses typically can.

### 3.5.1    *Reference point*

Have you ever gotten a great deal on eBay? It could be due to the seller's reference point. Sellers are often looking at value from when they acquired an item. This could range from free if they received the item as a gift, low cost if they found it at a yard sale, or very expensive if they paid top dollar and want to make a gain on their investment. If a seller had a large stash of collector's items given to them, they might set their reference point at zero dollars. That means anything above nothing is a gain. This seller is much more likely to set a low bid price and a low minimum acceptance price, and be happy making any money, particularly if selling items on eBay is not their full-time job.

Conversely, people who made a monetary investment, say in a concert ticket, know exactly what they paid. If the seller paid $40 per ticket, they are not going to feel happy about selling the ticket for $35. Even more, if the seller realizes the concert is sold out, they have the opportunity to view at what price others have been selling their tickets. Let's say the price is $100; this becomes the new anchor point. The seller will view more than $100 as a gain and less than as a loss.

The ability to look at what price similar items are selling is an affordance given to eBay and other online auctions that's much less effective if you're attending an auction in person and unable to monitor the results of auctions taking place in other rooms or different auction sites.

### 3.5.2   *The certainty effect and the scarcity heuristic*

eBay takes advantage of the certainty effect for both buyers and sellers to influence sales (figure 3.14). Many sales have a "buy now" price that allows users to immediately purchase a product. These items allow buyers and sellers to experience the certainty of the value of the sale, as opposed to the risk involved in letting users bid on an item. Allowing users to buy a product now eliminates the risk for both the seller who will sell the item at a guaranteed price, and the buyer who will know exactly what they will pay for the desired item.

The scarcity heuristic is evident in eBay's approach to showing how much time is left to bid on an item, as well as the quantity of an item and how many people have viewed the item per hour (figure 3.14). If a user likes a product that's almost out of stock and dozens of people have viewed it within the past hour, that user is more likely to place a bid or buy the product.

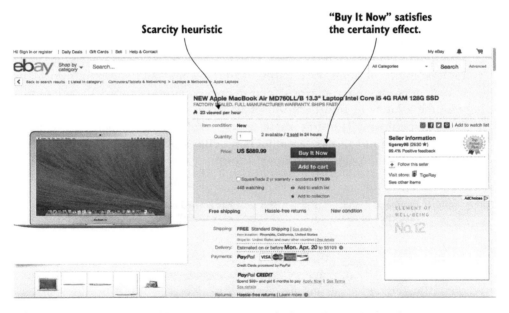

**Figure 3.14   eBay skillfully addresses both scarcity and certainty on its product pages.**

### 3.5.3   *The availability heuristic*

As eBay has grown, it has become synonymous with selling an item online. People say "sell that on eBay" or "I'd eBay that," when they're referring to the first thing that comes to mind as an example of a site for people selling goods online. Similar to the ease in which TurboTax is the first thing that comes to mind when my clients say they want to create an easy experience, eBay has inserted itself into availability of users' minds.

Even though now there are dozens of online auction sites, including Quibids and Beezid, and specialized sites like govedeals.com and nonprofits like Goodwill. You never hear someone say sell that thing on shopgoodwill.com! Today's featured collections again take advantage of the availability heuristic. People see an item or a collection on the homepage. They're more likely to view these items and consider purchasing if they didn't come to eBay for a specific purchase. Many of these items are familiar brands, which takes advantage of availability when people see something familiar.

### 3.5.4   *The familiarity heuristic*

Someone who has saved money on an eBay purchase is likely to use eBay again. So are folks who've found a rare item they needed to add to their collection. eBay is the default site when these people think of where their next savings or rarity will come from. Competitors would have a harder time convincing an eBay customer who experiences the familiarity heuristic than they would attempting to entice a new customer who hasn't used another site.

### 3.5.5   *Escalation of commitment*

eBay accounts for the escalation of commitment through the need to create an account for both buyers and sellers. Setting up an account is perhaps the most important thing for a user to do on eBay. Users with an account can track items and stores of interest, bid, sell items, save payment options, and save shipping information. eBay allows users who sell numerous items to create a store (figure 3.15). All of these users' customers know to find them on eBay; there would be a drastic cost to moving to another platform. The time these users spend uploading photos, creating product descriptions, and soliciting customers on eBay's platform would be a huge consideration against changing to another platform.

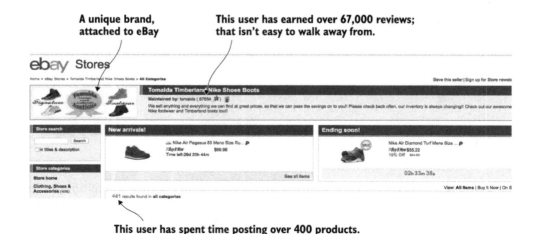

This user has spent time posting over 400 products.

**Figure 3.15   eBay offers users the ability to create stores—an escalation of commitment.**

### 3.5.6 *The scarcity heuristic*

eBay thrives on the concept of product scarcity. After all, an auction has only one winner. eBay didn't invent this concept. They moved it to a space that allowed many more people to view many more items considered scare. eBay is scalable beyond what potential brick-and-mortar auctions could ever be, in buyers, sellers, and profit for the auctioneer. eBay brings scarcity to another level, allowing bidders worldwide to compete for an item.

## 3.6 End-of-chapter exercise: Name that heuristic! and What's your product's sticky behavior?

Complete the following exercises to practice applying what you've learned in this chapter. You can share your answers and provide feedback on the Manning Publications forum here: https://forums.manning.com/forums/design-for-the-mind.

### 3.6.1 *Name that heuristic*

For each of the following, identify the heuristic being used:

1  You tell people your product is going to be the next Facebook of social media sites. You also design features that are similar to "Liking" and "Sharing" what other people are posting.

2  Your e-commerce site has "Midnight Specials" that last only an hour, and you show people how much stock is available for each product.

3  Your physician's online portal only displays pictures of male physicians and uses the terms "she" and "her" when referring to medical assistants and nurses.

4  You design an online banking experience that includes a feature showing users how many bills they've paid using online bill pay and auto-pay. You also display thank-you messages and provide special offers as people spend more time as customers (such as annually).

5  Your political news application allows users to rate each article they read as making them "Happy as a clam" or "Madder than hell." Each time a user selects one or the other, it starts to fill his clam-o-meter or mad-o-meter. When one of the meters begins to fill up faster, the display colors and language is changed to reflect the corresponding mood (that is, happy or mad).

6  You conduct a competitive analysis and determine navigation categories and the location of key design features for your product based on what your most successful competitors are doing.

### 3.6.2 *Sticky behaviors*

It's helpful to know what behaviors potential and new users need to engage in to become regular users of your product. You can then design to engage users in these behaviors earlier in the process. Use the following space to list the three most important behaviors your users need to engage in within the first few times they experience your product:

Now, schedule a meeting for your key team members to discuss these behaviors and answer the following questions:

- Does everyone agree these behaviors are the top three?
- How does your current design facilitate these behaviors?
- How could your current design improve the ability to engage users in these behaviors?

## 3.7    Additional resources

Barberis, N.C. (2012). *Thirty years of prospect theory in economics: A review and assessment* (No. w18621). Cambridge, MA: National Bureau of Economic Research. http://mng.bz/h9lh. (An article reviewing the achievements of research using prospect theory over the previous 30 years.)

Bloch, Blumberg, and Laartz (2012). Delivering large scale IT projects on time, on budget, and on value. McKinsey & Company http://mng.bz/Z513. (An article investigating the frequency of IT project failures, and the factors contributing to potential success.)

Camerer, C.F. (2004). Prospect theory in the wild: Evidence from the field. In C. F. Camerer, G. Loewenstein, and M. Rabin, eds., *Advances in Behavioral Economics*, 148–161. Princeton, NJ: Princeton University Press. (A deep exploration on the application of prospect theory, and the importance of accounting for psychology in economics and behavior.)

Kahneman, D., and A. Tversky. (1979). Prospect theory: An analysis of decision under risk. *Econometrica: Journal of the Econometric Society*, 47(2), 263–291. Available at http://bit.ly/1FN3k7c. (Kahneman and Tversky's seminal article introducing prospect theory.)

Yocco, V.S. (2015). Think fast! Using heuristics to increase use of your product. *Smashing Magazine*. Available at http://mng.bz/35F9. (An article I wrote on the application of additional heuristics not covered in this chapter.)

KEYWORDS: behavioral economics, heuristics, loss aversion, prospect theory, risk analysis

## 3.8    Summary

- Individuals make countless decisions each day, many of them with very little active thinking involved.
- Decisions under risk or uncertainty are decisions where the outcome isn't guaranteed.
- Editing and evaluation are the two key steps in making risky decisions.

- Editing involves ranking the potential outcomes from best to worst and determining which outcomes are worth considering.
- Evaluation involves determining which of the remaining outcomes is best, based on the value attached to the outcome, as well as the perceived probability of the outcome.
- People enter a situation with a reference point—they'll determine if a decision leads to a loss or a gain based on this reference point.
- Heuristics, or mental shortcuts, help people make decisions quickly; researchers have identified many heuristics people regularly use.
- Loss aversion suggests that people experience great displeasure from a loss and therefore look to avoid losing.
- The certainty effect states that people are more likely to take a certain gain for less than one that's only likely but more than the certain gain.
- The disposition effect states that people cash in on gains too quickly and hold on to losses for too long.
- The availability heuristic states that people assign the choice that comes to mind the quickest the highest value.
- The affect heuristic states that the emotion people are feeling when they make a decision will influence that decision.
- The familiarity heuristic states that people think outcomes from past decisions will remain consistent with the same decisions in the future.
- Escalation of commitment occurs when individuals stick with a decision because of the amount of time or money they've already invested in it.
- The scarcity heuristic suggests that people are more likely to think something has value if there are limited quantities or it's considered exclusive.

# Motivation, ability, and trigger—boom!

Jonathan has just received a job in a different country. He's excited for the opportunity and knows it'll be beneficial to learn a new language. He uses the internet to research the opportunities to take a class in the local community college, do a distance-learning program delivered online, or download a language-learning application that's compatible with his tablet and smartphone. The next morning, Jonathan wakes up, checks his email on his iPad, and finds a discount code to download the tablet- and smartphone-based application. He clicks the link and downloads the application. Why did Jonathan choose to go with the app-based language-learning system? The principle of motivation, ability, and trigger (figure 4.1) tells us that he received the email offer (the trigger) at exactly the right moment when his motivation and ability to purchase the app were high.

So far, we've covered two principles of psychology focusing on what leads to planned behavior and what contributes to making decisions under risk. Let's continue our exploration of designing for behavior by examining how we might use technology, specifically digital design, to facilitate behavior and behavior change.

**NOTE** The principle of planned behavior we explored in chapter 2 shows us how to account for well-thought-out behaviors. Decisions under risk from chapter 3 complements these behaviors with the more spontaneous behaviors (loss aversion and heuristics) and those that lead to a gain or loss.

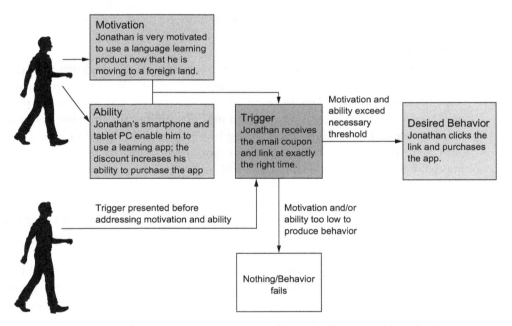

**Figure 4.1  Motivation, ability, and trigger need to unfold in a logical way to promote a behavior.**

Here we look at motivation, ability, and trigger to explain when we should ask users to engage in a behavior (use our site, click this button), and how we facilitate getting them to the point they say "Yes!" Figure 4.1 shows that users first encounter features designed to increase motivation and ability to engage in a behavior for the trigger to be successful. If a design presents the trigger (call to action) before motivation and ability reach sufficiently high levels, or presents the trigger before addressing motivation and ability, the behavior won't occur.

## 4.1    Introduction

How can you design your product so that it presents an opportunity for users to engage in a behavior at the right moment? Motivation, ability, and trigger is a simple principle—perhaps too simple for academia, which makes it perfect for us. According to motivation, ability, and trigger, behavior happens when a person

- Is motivated
- Has the ability to engage in the behavior
- Is effectively presented with a trigger that will cause the behavior

That's it. Let's call it a day and head home. But wait, there's more!

These three elements must align at the right moment for the intended behavior to occur. Ideally, individuals are highly motivated and have the ability to easily engage in the behavior the moment you present them with a trigger. The principle is based on Fogg's Behavioral Model, which describes how to use technology to influence behavior.

### 4.1.1    Brief academic background

B.J. Fogg and his colleagues at Stanford's persuasive technology lab provide us with the foundation for this chapter's principle. In the 1990s, Fogg was curious to explain how we can use technology to change behavior. He realized technology, particularly web-based experiences, was opening up new possibilities for thinking about influencing behavior. He examined the existing psychological literature on behavior change and identified the key factors of motivation, ability, and trigger, which became his model. Fogg noted that technology itself isn't the cure-all for explaining behavior. A person won't magically start taking pictures because they have a photo app on their phone. Users need to understand why they should use the app and when they should use the app, and the app needs to be presented correctly and at the right time. As Fogg states on his website, "[technology is] simply a channel for delivering an experience. And you must get the experience right."

Research on persuasive technology has focused on what elements need to be present for humans to develop relationships with technology. In one study, Fogg and his colleagues manipulated how computers communicated with users, through either a dominant or a subordinate personality. Participants needed to work with the computer to determine how to survive being stranded in the desert. A computer with a dominant personality had traits such as bold typography and made statements with an authoritative tone such as, "In the desert, the intense sunlight will clearly cause blindness by the second day. The sunglasses are absolutely necessary." Contrast this with the submissive computer that would make suggestions like, "The sunglasses might be important."

The researchers found that people strongly preferred to work with the computer that matched their personality. Participants judged the computers with similar personalities as more competent, and the interaction as more beneficial than participants using a computer with a misaligned personality did. Researchers use these findings to provide evidence that we can use technology to persuade people. Researchers and practitioners can now use persuasive technology to help inform our efforts to make people more efficient or healthier through mobile and wearable technology.

Persuasive technology is a young field and reflects the reality of the situation it's growing up in. Academics and philosophers have always theorized on technology and its effects, but Fogg's is a model born and raised in the digital age. Seventy-five years ago, Fogg or another academic wouldn't have been thinking about how principles of psychology would apply to digital design on computer and smartphone screens. They might have been more likely to look at the impact of radio and telephone becoming ubiquitous in homes.

TurboTax provides a great example of the application of motivation, ability, and trigger in design. Individuals are pretty highly motivated to file taxes, even if they don't like it. They'll receive large fines and other potential penalties if they fail to file taxes. But not many people find it easy to understand the U.S. Tax Code.

TurboTax (figure 4.2) ltakes advantage of this motivation and makes up for this lack of ability by simplifying the process. TurboTax increases users' ability to find the correct product and file taxes by asking them simple questions using everyday terminology (for example, did you have a child this year?). TurboTax motivates users by allowing them to go through the workflows associated with creating tax documents, but then asking for payment before granting access to the completed forms and official IRS submission. They also offer the option to purchase the software immediately. Having these two trigger points is a good strategy. People who have familiarity with the product can purchase it up front, whereas those on the fence can get a realistic feel for the value the product provides (increased ability), before agreeing to make the purchase in order to receive the benefit.

Let's take a closer look at the different elements of motivation, ability, and trigger.

**Figure 4.2   TurboTax increases ability where motivation is already high.**

## 4.2    Key concepts of motivation, ability, and trigger

You won't find many situations that naturally involve the perfect mix of high motivation, high ability, and an effectively presented trigger. You can do many things to help increase one area or all three.

### What a mess! The butcher, the baker, and the candlestick maker

Once upon a time, there were three entrepreneurs: a butcher, a baker, and a candlestick maker. Each one received money from a venture capitalist. Each one had a great product design.

**Lack of ability**

The *butcher* traveled to a number of well-attended lunch and dinner events and presented the wealthy attendees with free samples of her choicest cuts of meat. She did this just before the start of the event, when attendees were most hungry.

People trying the meats stated they wanted to immediately place an order. "You can't order these here today. I don't have any way for you to place an order," the butcher told potential customers. Instead, she provided them with a card containing her web address and the name of her tablet/mobile application.

Later, attendees failed to remember their encounter with the butcher, others were so full of food it no longer sounded appetizing to place an order, and others just didn't feel as inspired about the meats as they had after tasting them.

**Lack of motivation**

The *baker* took a different approach to growing his business. He showed up at large dinner affairs with his goods. The baker had the ability to take orders and process sales on the spot. Everyone wanted to know how they could order them and when they could receive them. "What luck!" said the baker, "I've brought my entire stock of fresh-baked goods here with me tonight." Unfortunately, most people chose not to make a purchase, because they were no longer hungry after the event.

**No trigger**

The *candlestick maker* hosted her own special event. She let attendees use her candles to take candlelight tours of the beautiful gardens on the grounds of the facility hosting the event. She also let people burn candles in order to get a sense of how they'd smell. At the end of what seemed like an extremely successful event, the candlestick maker collapsed with a sigh onto a couch. "Well, what were our sales like?" she asked her assistant. "Sales? What sales? We didn't ask anyone to purchase the candles."

A month later, the venture capitalist summoned the three entrepreneurs to her office. "You have all failed miserably," she said. "Butcher: you had people extremely motivated to purchase your product, but you failed to provide them with the ability to do so at the appropriate time. Baker: you had your entire product ready and able to go. But nobody was motivated to order more food after indulging in a dinner event. Candlestick maker: You had people excited to buy your product, you had all of your product ready to go and in the right place, and you completely failed to offer any of it for sale. People didn't know how or if they could purchase your candles."

**The moral of the story:** Each entrepreneur had a product that met the needs of potential users. Each failed to incorporate one of the key concepts of ability, motivation, and trigger. You need to account for all three if you want to cause a user to engage in the behavior you desire, with the least amount of resistance.

### 4.2.1　*People need motivation to complete a task*

*Motivation* provides a reason for someone to engage in a behavior. It can be intrinsic, coming from within, such as when people are motivated by a sense of accomplishment. Motivation can also be extrinsic, or external, such as when people are motivated by getting money or praise.

Temple Run (figure 4.3) and Temple Run 2 users have downloaded the smartphone games over 1 billion times combined. This number is a good indicator that the designers have effectively motivated users to download and play the games. The never-ending games motivate users to continue playing in an effort to make it further in the game than they have, to unlock (sometimes through in-app purchases) secret items, and for bragging rights among friends and other gamers. Players are motivated by the pleasure they feel playing the game and the hope to continue reaching higher levels. Motivation is a critical component to any digital property that goes viral.

People are motivated by a number of things, including

**Figure 4.3　Temple Run has motivated over a billion downloads and nearly 2 million ratings.**

- *Pleasure or pain*—People are motivated by the opportunity to experience pleasure or avoid pain.
- *Hope and fear*—People are motivated to engage in behaviors that increase hope and reduce fear.
- *Social acceptance and social rejection*—People are often driven by the desire to be socially accepted and avoid social rejection.

Motivation is a complex concept and the three pairs listed here just begin to scratch the surface. Other motivators include alertness and exhaustion, financial loss or gain, praise or admonishment, and rewards such as food, money, and sex.

### 4.2.2   *People need the ability to complete the task*

GrubHub (figure 4.4) is an example of a product that increases ability. Hunger is already motivating users. GrubHub reduces the time it takes to find local restaurants that are open, reduces physical effort by showing which ones deliver, and reduces the amount of thinking by allowing users to filter using a number of categories.

Factors contributing to ability include

- *Time*—Everyone wants more of it and no one has enough.
- *Money*—People with limited resources might find price to be a barrier, with a reduction in price leading to increased ability.
- *Physical effort*—The more physical effort users need to put forth, the more demanding the task.
- *Mental effort*—The more thinking needed to understand how to do or use something, the more difficult the behavior.
- *Social acceptability*—It's easier for people to engage in socially acceptable behaviors.
- *Routine*—People are better able to engage in behaviors that can become or are routine.

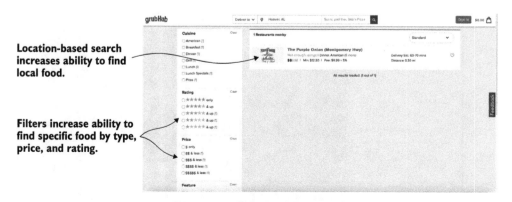

Location-based search increases ability to find local food.

Filters increase ability to find specific food by type, price, and rating.

**Figure 4.4   GrubHub increases users' ability to find and order food for delivery ... unless it happens to be 10:45 p.m. in Hoover, Ala; then you won't find GrubHub that helpful.**

### 4.2.3 People need triggers to engage in the task

Triggers tell a person to do something. We typically refer to these as a call to action in digital design. Without triggers, a person wouldn't be aware of or able to engage in a behavior. Triggers must be presented once motivation and ability have reached sufficiently high levels for the person to engage in a behavior. For example, Google offers a free trial of their Cloud Platform (figure 4.5). They allow users to build ability and motivation to use their product over the course of the free trial. Once the trial ends, they'll present the trigger: the option to purchase the product.

**Figure 4.5   Google Cloud Platform presents users with the trigger to "Start your free trial." When the trial ends, they'll present the trigger to purchase access to the product.**

The principle of motivation, ability, and trigger identifies three types of triggers (aka calls to action) for a behavior. The three types of triggers are

- *Facilitator*—A facilitator assists a person engage in a behavior. The tool tips we encounter when completing online forms are an example of a facilitator.
- *Spark*—A spark provides a boost to a person's motivation. An email with a limited time discount or early access to a product is a spark.
- *Signal*—Signals are a less assertive type of trigger. Signals can apply to each of our senses. For example, the Ding! sound of an incoming instant message lets users know they won't be wasting time if they check for a new message in the near future.

Triggers play a critical role in determining when or even if behaviors might occur.

## 4.3   How to design for motivation, ability, and trigger

The principle of motivation, ability, and trigger provides a lot of relevant information for you to digest. The principle highlights the need to constantly examine how we're building up our users' motivation and ability before we ask them to engage in a behavior. Let's take a closer look at how you can apply the concepts of the principle to your work.

### 4.3.1   Increasing motivation

Many design techniques can be motivational. Researchers have identified two types of motivation:

- *Extrinsic motivation*—Extrinsic motivation comes from the outside or external forces. Examples include money, public praise, a promotion, or having a pizza party.
- *Intrinsic motivation*—Intrinsic motivation comes from within an individual. Examples include curiosity to learn something and the satisfaction of solving a problem or achieving a goal.

Offering a combination of extrinsic and intrinsic motivators is the best strategy. Examples include offering a discount (extrinsic motivation to save money) and providing an experience that becomes easier to do over time, such as learning a new skill or healthy habit (intrinsic hope for achieving a goal).

#### PLEASURE AND PAIN

You account for pleasure when you design a usable experience. You should engage in usability testing and interviews to identify the areas of your product that cause pleasure or contribute to pain in an experience.

Additionally, you should identify the opportunities to highlight the pleasure your product can cause. Eventbrite's mobile application (figure 4.6) allows users to find pleasurable events to attend via their smartphones. Eventbrite highlights what you can do with the app throughout their online experience. Users can find and attend events their friends and peers are attending (social acceptance). Users also avoid the pain of losing or forgetting an event ticket, as they're able to access their tickets directly from the app.

**Figure 4.6   Eventbrite motivates users to find and attend pleasurable events, and avoid the rejection of missing an event.**

**HOPE AND FEAR**

Your design should inspire hope and/or reduce fear. How does your product inspire hope? If you're running a dating website, your users are hopeful to find a date or meet a long-term partner. You would want to focus on facilitating these types of interactions over ones that distract users from these goals. If you're creating a discount electronics e-commerce site, users are inspired by the hope they'll find a good deal. You can also account for hope through the following components of design:

- *Simple navigation*—Users hope they can find what they're looking for.
- *Clear jargon-free terminology, side-by-side comparison of products*—Users hope they choose the correct product.
- *Progress bars and straightforward error messages*—Users hope they'll complete the task they engaged in.
- *Clearly displaying the benefits of using your product*—Users hope your product leaves them better off than their current state.

**SOCIAL ACCEPTANCE AND REJECTION**

You want to convey the impression to potential users that using your product is socially acceptable. You can include many features that will create and reflect social acceptance of your product:

- Allow users to share links directly to your product
- Display the number of times the product link has been shared
- Encourage product reviews
- Include links to reviewing your product in the receipt emailed to users
- Text users a link to post a review once they've used your product
- Strategically place requests for users to review your product

Your design can also facilitate users avoiding social rejection. Some examples of design features that help our users avoid social rejection are as follows:

- Timely alerts to breaking news and information (stay as informed as your peers)
- Event reminders (meet your obligations)
- Creating and sharing group values (creating common terminology and common interests)

Feel free to add more motivators as you see fit. Your goals should be to identify the motivators that are positive in nature, and how your design addresses or activates these motivators.

### 4.3.2 *Increasing ability*

Digital designs and products should inherently increase the ability of your users over the nondigital version. Take a mobile phone application for the game solitaire (figure 4.7). An app removes the need for a deck of cards, a playing space, shuffling, and keeping score. Users now have the ability play cards in any space they can use their phone.

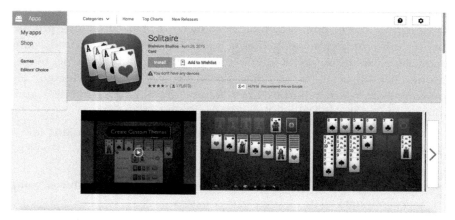

**Figure 4.7   Board game apps turn users' mobile device into an arcade or card table.**

### HOW TO DESIGN FOR ABILITY

Your product should increase both the ability for users to accomplish the task it's designed for, as well as users' ability to use the actual product (simple to use). If it takes users longer to find the shirt they want on your e-commerce clothing site than it would for them to drive to the mall and buy the same shirt, you're failing to increase your users' ability.

You need to identify which resources are scarcest for users, and how you can address them in your design:

- If users have plenty of time but not much money, offer them a DIY way to make or save money with your product.
- If users have plenty of money and little time, offer them a way to accomplish the task quicker by paying extra.
- If you find that users are thinking too hard or your product is confusing, conduct card sorts, interviews, usability testing, and other UX research methods to determine how you should categorize content, label fields, and provide FAQs.

Good user experience respects the time and effort a user needs to spend to learn and use a product.

---

#### Forms, damn forms, and digital forms

No one likes filling out forms. Here's a list of some fatal flaws you need to avoid in any experience requiring users to complete a form:

- *Asking for information users don't have readily available*—Provide users with a list of the information they'll need immediately at the instruction page of the form.

- *Using inconsistent/unclear field labels*—Emailing users an «Access Code», for example, but then labeling the form field «Password». You'll confuse users and generate calls to your support center if you fail to provide clear form labels.
- *Losing the affordances of paper*—Users are accustomed to paper forms where they can skip irrelevant questions, go back and change answers on a whim, and take their time to complete. You should include logic in any form you create, skipping questions that become unnecessary based on user response, or at least allow users to skip these questions.
- *Failing to capitalize on the benefits of digital*—Many digital forms fail to prepopulate data. Similarly, if a user already has one type of account with your product, they should have the opportunity to import all relevant information into form fields when opening up a new type of account or product.

Forms require designs that delicately balance maintaining the positive affordances of the physical version, and integrating the enhancements that digital designs allow.

### 4.3.3　*Presenting effective triggers*

Triggers are only effective when motivation and ability have reached critical mass. Let's review examples of the three types of triggers we've discussed:

- *Facilitator*—The user should be in a position to begin proficient use once encountering the facilitator. NBC Sports provides users with an overlay (figure 4.8) that shows users where critical functions are placed and how to use them. NBC Sports wants to trigger the behavior of using their product and the updated features.

**Figure 4.8　NBC Sports Network facilitates an easy and fun way to learn the location and functionality of key features available to online viewers.**

- *Signal*—There are limitless potential signals. Our job is to learn which ones are more effective in specific contexts and around specific behaviors. Signals are audible, visual, or other sense-related cues that tell a person to do something. A call to action button, such as Amazon's "Add to Cart" (figure 4.9), presented within a product description is an example of a signal; it lets users learn about the product, and then gives them the signal to make the purchase.

A call to action to add to cart is a signal-type trigger.

**Figure 4.9    Amazon presents users with a signal to purchase the product on each product's page.**

- *Sparks*—Sparks are good for stimulating brief and simple behaviors. You can send alerts, tweets, status updates, and notifications directly to users' devices. Allowing users to easily share a message, such as retweeting directly from their mobile phone (figure 4.10), is an example of a simple and common spark trigger.

Retweet and quote tweet are triggers to engage in a simple behavior—information sharing—without requiring high level of ability.

Figure 4.10    Retweeting a coupon code is a simple behavior sparked by users checking Twitter on their mobile devices.

**HOW TO DESIGN FOR TRIGGERS**

Users need to be aware of the trigger, understand that the trigger will result in engaging in the desired behavior, and be above the threshold of motivation and ability in order to activate the trigger and engage in the behavior. You address effective triggers in your design when you

- Present clearly labeled jargon-free calls to action
- Place calls to action throughout an experience, particularly after providing users with motivation and ability
- Make the call to action relevant to the topic of the page
- Place the call to action for actions like submit, purchase, and continue, in the appropriate context or location of the workflow
- Visually distinguish calls to action from other types of information on the page

> **The value of patience: When the heck can I present the trigger?**
>
> We are an impatient bunch: We want to convert our potential users into power users overnight. We want our trial version customers to purchase pro accounts in less than a week.
>
> Motivation, ability, and trigger give us insight into the importance of well-placed triggers. Often, you'll have multiple opportunities to present users with triggers. You'll benefit if you base the presentation of these triggers on behavioral data from users and the timing is in line with high levels of motivation and ability.

### 4.3.4　*Mobile design increases ability*

Each concept we've covered in this chapter applies equally to mobile designs. Mobile delivery inherently increases the ability of many users. Here are examples:

- Banking mobile apps allow for checking balance and depositing checks anywhere with a connection, and in less time than calling customer service or visiting a branch.
- Calendar and to-do list apps remove the need to carry around a physical day planner, can alert users audibly and physically (vibration) to an upcoming appointment, and don't require erasing when plans change.
- Map applications replace the need to carry around a map, print directions, or own a separate GPS system in your car.
- Video chat apps allow users to view their friends and colleagues while having a conversation from anywhere with a fast enough connection. Users can give their loved one a virtual tour of their new house in real time from thousands of miles away.
- Food and grocery applications deliver location-based offers at times users might be hungry.

Your design should account for mobile, tablet, and wearable technology experiences.

Beacon technology provides an example of how the future might look for mobile design. Beacons are meant to trigger a behavior at the exact time users are most motivated and able, while they're standing in a store looking at a product. Real-time, geographically based triggers provide an exciting opportunity to influence user behavior. Users can expect to set a reminder based on location and not time (such as "remind me to buy a new wig next time I'm within 500 feet of a wig shop"). Users will view these reminders as respectful of their time and resources, allowing designs that include them to outshine their competition.

## 4.4   *Talking the talk: conversations about motivation, ability, and trigger*

Concepts of motivation, ability, and trigger provide an easy way to discuss elements of your design with clients or others involved with your project. Let's say you're redesigning a client's website for their data visualization product. The site currently requires all potential users to register before viewing more information or videos of the product in use. Your redesign will reflect concerns you heard from their potential users that they didn't want to create an account before having an opportunity to see the product in action.

- *Discussing how you've addressed motivation*—"We have relocated examples of user created output from behind the login to having its own navigation category on the .com homepage. When potential users view this output, they see a label displaying how long it took them to make the visualization, what they listed as their level of experience with creating visualizations, and if available, testimonials from users who created images. We believe this will increase potential users' motivation to create a basic account."

- *Discussing how you've addressed ability*—"We've relocated some of the how-to and demo videos to be accessible before users are required to log in. We've added templates for a number of additional visualizations we heard potential users say they'd like to have available. We've also renamed the navigation categories to remove terms users felt were jargon. We've done this so that we increase potential users' ability to create an account and potentially purchase the product *after* they're exposed to the increased ability your product will give them."

- *Discussing how you've addressed triggers*—"We've added a number of additional areas where users can pull the trigger on purchasing your product. We'd like to highlight one specific addition: we now allow users to enter their own data and create a visualization using a template provided without having purchased the product. The output contains a watermark that says 'Free Trial' as well as deactivating the ability to update field names or labels. We then present users with a call to action to purchase access, which will take users to the product order workflow. You can see from the examples that we already use terminology from the principle of technology and behavior in our everyday conversations. Your clients and colleagues won't need an interpreter to understand these words. Plus, who doesn't want a reason to get to say the word 'trigger' more often?"

## 4.5    *Case study: Fitbit*

Fitbit creates wearable technology that tracks users' physical stats and performance (such as calories burned in a day, steps taken, and time spent sleeping). Fitbit has positioned itself as a leader in health and fitness wearable technology. Fitbit's products and success are a reflection of the benefit of shaping your design with the key components of the principle of motivation, ability, and trigger.

Fitbit sells their hardware to users, allowing them to utilize Fitbit's mobile application to record data, or maintain the use of one of many compatible apps. Fitbit provides software in the form of desktop (figure 4.11) and mobile applications that address each component of motivation, ability, and trigger.

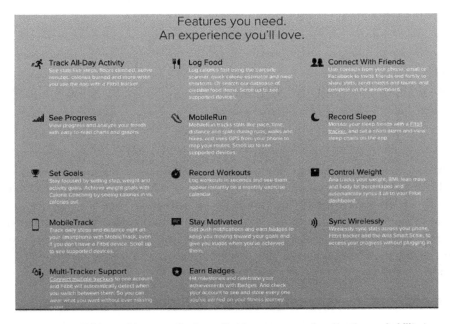

**Figure 4.11    Fitbit provides many features that increase users' motivation and ability to use their product, as well as to engage in healthier behaviors.**

**MOTIVATION**

The Fitbit application and wearable unit allow users to

- Feel hope that they'll increase healthy behaviors, learn more about their current health status, and improve their health if needed
- Avoid fear of the consequences of unhealthy lifestyle choices
- Maintain intrinsic motivation by setting and achieving goals that also build up physical endurance as users work toward them
- Gain social acceptance and avoid rejection through users' social networks
- Earn badges reflecting specific physical accomplishments

**ABILITY**

Fitbit increases ability by

- Removing barriers of time in delivering the messages directly to the users, in the context of their day (time to run!)
- Reducing mental effort in allowing users to record their activity and food intake directly on the mobile application
- Providing messages in line with the preexisting routine of carrying a phone and/or wearing an unobtrusive and comfortable device
- Opting users in to alerts that remind them to eat healthy around meal or snack times
- Providing alarms with reminders to promote users' engagement in healthy behavior
- Transmitting wirelessly user statistics, removing the need to remember to plug in the product to a computer

**TRIGGER**

Fitbit presents users with multiple triggers throughout their product's design:

- Friends can send messages or taunts.
- Fitbit can send alerts as reminders to users.
- Users can see how close they are to achieving a daily goal.

Fitbit is providing technology that will serve as a base for many future wearable devices and concepts. They've already expanded to other types of products, including a scale that syncs information with the application. We should see an increase in similar devices that will monitor users' health in real time, transmitting data to relevant sources such as doctors or emergency rooms. Fitbit is an example of how wearables addressing motivation, ability, and trigger might successfully facilitate the desired behaviors and generate use of a product.

## 4.6    *End-of-chapter exercise: motivation, ability, and trigger*

We've covered the three main components of motivation, ability, and trigger in this chapter. Let's review your understanding of each component, and then have a design challenge.

### 4.6.1    *Motivation, ability, or trigger*

For each question, choose which component of motivation, ability, and trigger is missing. You can share your answers and provide feedback on the Manning Publications forum at https://forums.manning.com/forums/design-for-the-mind:

- You provide customers with a 30-day free trial of your product. They really enjoy the product and want to purchase the full version. You fail to follow up with offers to purchase the product during the free trial period.

  Motivation    Ability    Trigger

- Users can find extensive information on your cause to reduce air pollution, but you don't present them with an argument for what they should do next. Users encounter multiple "Donate now" links but they don't understand why they should.
  Motivation   Ability   Trigger

- Users are able to view testimonials from others about how great your product is, but when they see the price of your product, they're unable to afford the expense. You then ask them to buy it now.
  Motivation   Ability   Trigger

- Your customers need to convert all of their data collection to digital formats, but the digital form for collecting data is more complicated than the print version.
  Motivation   Ability   Trigger

- Users fail to see how your product will help them accomplish their goals. They can easily download a free trial, but this doesn't seem to help convert them to users.
  Motivation   Ability   Trigger

### 4.6.2   *Design challenge: wearable technology to achieve better health*

Preventing or changing disease-promoting behaviors such as smoking or overeating has been a quill in the snout of public health officials for decades. Organizations like the Centers for Disease Control (CDC) want people to quit smoking, drink in moderation, get cancer screenings on a regular schedule, and eat a well-balanced diet.

We're starting to see products like Fitbit and other wearable technology (combined with mobile applications like MyFitnessPal) gain traction in use to promote diet and exercise. Your mission for this design challenge is to create the design of both the wearable technology and the accompanying application that will help users who smoke cigarettes kick the habit. You'll need to include each component of motivation, ability, and trigger. Feel free to recruit your colleagues to help with the design.

Provide a brief description of your wearable product and the accompanying application to complete the design challenge:

- How does your product address *motivation?*


- How does your product address *ability?*


- How would your product address the needs of a 65-year-old user who has smoked two packs a day for 50 years?

- How would your product address the needs of a 20-year-old smoker who has smoked up to five cigarettes a day for the past year?

- How might your product prevent users who don't currently smoke from starting?

- How might your product assist users who have quit smoking maintain their non-smoker status?

## 4.7    Additional resources

Fogg, B.J. (2002). Persuasive technology: Using computers to change what we think and do. *Ubiquity*, 2002 (December), 5. (A report on a number of studies Fogg and his colleagues conducted on persuasive technology.)

——————. (2009, April). A behavior model for persuasive design. In S. Chatterjee and P. Dev, eds., *Proceedings of the 4th international Conference on Persuasive Technology* (p. 40). ACM. (Fogg introduces his model for using technology to influence behavior.)

Fogg, B.J. and J. Hreha. (2010). Behavior wizard: A method for matching target behaviors with solutions. In T. Ploug, P. Halse, and H. Oinas-Kukkonen, eds., *Persuasive Technology* (pp. 117–131). Springer: Berlin Heidelberg. (Fogg provides guidance for how to use technology to influence specific behaviors.)

KEYWORDS: call to action, extrinsic motivation, Fogg's behavioral model, intrinsic motivation, persuasive technology

## 4.8    Summary

- Motivation, ability, and trigger are the three key components to determining a user's behavior.
- Motivation and ability must reach a specific threshold for the trigger to elicit the desired behavior.
- Your design should address extrinsic motivation such as money, rewards, or public praise, and intrinsic motivation such as hope and a sense of accomplishment.
- You design to increase ability when you ensure your design is usable, accomplishes tasks quickly, and is in line with users' mental models.
- Facilitator, signal, and spark are three types of commonly used triggers.
- Facilitator triggers assist users in completing a task; for example, contextual help on a form.

- Signal triggers are calls to action that apply to user's senses, such as an Add to Cart icon.
- Spark triggers provide a quick boost to a user's motivation; for example, a 24-hour-only sale! icon.
- Mobile and wearable technology provide good opportunities to send users triggers while they're engaging in specific behaviors.

# Part 3

## Principles of influence and persuasion: not as evil as you'd think

This part of the book will introduce you to principles directly tied to influence and persuasion. You won't learn how to be a good used-car salesperson. Rather, you'll learn how to meet your users' needs by incorporating elements of influence and persuasion into your product's design.

Chapter 5 provides everything you need to know to address influence using research-supported techniques. You'll see that much of what we call good design already accounts for influence. You'll now understand why this is true, and you'll see how to identify where your product will benefit from designing for influence.

Chapter 6 expands our discussion into the realm of social influence. People are inherently social, and your design should reflect this. You'll learn about the importance of social influence techniques that help make people feel closer to the groups they belong to and less like the groups they don't feel part of. You'll understand the importance of connecting people through your product, as well as making opportunities for reviewing your product easy for users.

Chapter 7 focuses on how we frame communication with our users. You'll learn how to craft well-framed communication in this chapter. Communication is much more than words. You can use experiences, pictures, sound, symbols, and more to communicate with your users. You'll need to carefully consider how, when, and why you communicate with users. Framing involves setting the tone of how you want users to interpret your message, including what action you want them to take. You can say the same thing in many different ways to best communicate with the greatest number of users.

Chapter 8 presents a research-based model for how persuasion works. The Elaboration Likelihood Model explains that people are persuaded through deep processing of information as well as peripheral information, such as the credibility they give the source of the message. You'll learn how to address both of these methods of persuasion with your product's design.

# Influence: getting people to like and use your design

**This chapter covers**

- Understanding the principle of influence
- Ensuring your design accommodates the principle of influence
- Identifying opportunities to design to influence users
- Discussing influence with others
- Applying the principle of influence in digital design contexts

Francine watches birds as one of her hobbies. One day, she sees a rarely sighted bird as she's walking to her car after work. She whips out her smartphone and takes a perfect picture of the bird as it's in flight. She then posts the picture to Instagram so all her birder friends can see what she came across. When Francine arrives home, she sees that a number of people have liked and shared her picture. Some of them she has never even met. Francine feels proud of her picture and feels like she wants to express her appreciation to everyone who shared her photo. She logs in to Instagram and finds a photo to share from each person who shared her photo; even people she

93

never met before, even photos she isn't really that interested in sharing. Francine has just engaged in reciprocity: she received something and then felt obligated to do something in return, one of the key concepts of the principle of influence.

This chapter will introduce the principle of influence to kick off our discussion on influence and persuasion. Influence (figure 5.1) taps into our ability to shape the attitudes and behaviors of others toward our product. We see influence at work in our everyday lives, from how we convince our peers to work with us, to what products we purchase, to what websites and applications we use. Everything we encounter has the potential to influence us.

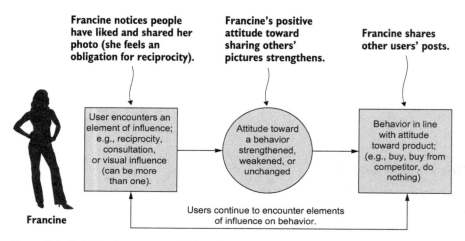

**Figure 5.1   Individuals encounter an element of influence that positively or negatively impacts their attitude or leaves it unchanged. Individuals then engage in a behavior in line with the attitude. The process happens repeatedly as we come across elements of influence throughout our daily life.**

You must proactively address influence in your designs, or you'll lose users to other more influential designs. Fortunately, the opposite is true as well. You gain users when you effectively incorporate influence in your design.

## 5.1    Introduction

Since the day we are born, other people influence us. Our parents or caregiver influenced what we ate and drank, whom we visited, and where we lived. Our exposure to other people through school or activities led to additional encounters with influence. We often credit salespeople who are influential with being good at sales. In reality, sometimes we're subjected to influence because we don't care to do the work of forming an opinion about something ourselves, and sometimes it's because someone or something is effectively using the principle of influence. Your design needs to account for influencing users in either one of these mind-sets.

Most of us are also attempting to influence others on a daily basis. We wanted to influence our employer or client to hire us, we want to influence our children to clean their bedrooms, and we want to influence our talented colleagues to work with us on a difficult project. I want to influence you to read this book and recommend it to others. Influence is an important part of all our lives.

### 5.1.1 *Academic background*

Harvard University professor Herbert Kelman is responsible for providing the foundation for much of the research on influence in which today's academics engage. Kelman wanted to understand more about why people hold inconsistent attitudes, particularly in stressful situations. He noticed that many people express one attitude in public but hold a different attitude when asked privately.

Kelman's research identified three processes of influence. He had groups of people engage in tasks such as reading essays and listening to speeches on various political topics. He then asked them to report their attitudes about a topic on which they'd already given him information about their attitude. Kelman found individuals changed their attitudes through one of three ways:

- *Compliance*—Individuals will agree with the attitudes of others in public but state differing opinions in private. In one study, Kelman presented 7th-grade students with a message about comic books that conflicted with the view they held (groups of students stating they liked comic books received a message that reading comic books was bad). Participants then wrote a brief essay stating their view on reading comics. An instructor encouraged one group of participants to conform with the view of the conflicting message they'd received. The other group didn't receive such coaching. The group that received encouragement to conform wrote more essays agreeing with the conflicting view, but fewer of those participants expressed a true change of attitude toward comic book reading when asked privately.
- *Identification*—Individuals' attitudes are influenced by someone they identify with or find attractive. Kelman had people listen to recordings about topics related to a U.S. Supreme Court decision on desegregating schools. Study participants who identified with the speaker stated stronger agreement with the speaker's viewpoint than with participants who didn't identify with the speaker.
- *Internalization*—Individuals process information they find important and develop an attitude they hold both publicly and privately. Kelman found that attitudes are most consistent when people receive information from sources they found credible and they're able to express their attitudes in private. Kelman concluded that source credibility was the contributing factor leading to this type of influence.

Kelman used his research to help develop psychotherapy programs at Johns Hopkins University. He felt an understanding of his three processes of influence could enhance the relationship between group therapy members and counselors, leading to better outcomes. Kelman also applied his work to understanding how and why people identify with and become active as members of their communities.

More recently, Arizona State University professor Robert Cialdini has spent a lifetime and a successful career identifying techniques people use to influence each other. Cialdini was originally motivated to research influence because he wanted to learn more about why people often blur the lines of their power into misuse or abuse. Cialdini, however, has shared his knowledge for the power of good.

Cialdini and his colleagues have conducted a number of studies to understand how influence works. One study found people are more likely to say yes to a small commitment after first being asked to make a large commitment to which they say no. Researchers approached participants to ask them if they'd be willing to volunteer to chaperone a trip of children from a juvenile detention center to the local zoo (a small commitment). One group of participants was asked if they'd be willing to spend the summer as an unpaid intern at a county juvenile detention center (a large commitment) prior to being asked if they'd commit to the small commitment task. Researchers asked another group only to make the small commitment, and one additional group was presented with both options simultaneously and told they could choose either (or neither).

The researchers found a large and significant difference in commitment to the small task for people that they asked to engage in the large commitment task first. Fifty percent of the people from the large commitment first group agreed to engage in the small commitment task, compared to 25% in the "choose either or neither" group and less than 17% in the small commitment-only group. No participants agreed to the large commitment task. Cialdini concluded that people develop a sense of reciprocity (covered in this chapter) or obligation after saying no to someone asking them to engage a large task that leaves them more likely to comply with being asked to engage in a smaller task (called the "door-in-the-face" technique, covered in section 6.3.3). They conducted a number of additional studies that confirmed their initial findings.

Cialdini's research informs everything from how fortune 500 CEOs run their companies to how environmentalists frame messages meant to help promote environment-friendly behaviors. Along the way, Cialdini has written multiple best-selling books to help others learn to apply his techniques of influence.

## 5.2   Key concepts of influence

Researchers have identified many tactics under the umbrella of "influence." Cialdini published an extremely popular book on influence covering what he described as six "weapons" for influencing people. I cover two of Cialdini's ferocious tactics in this chapter:

- *Commitment and consistency*—People desire to follow through on commitments they've made.
- *Reciprocity*—People don't like feeling in debt to others; they seek to return favors.

I covered Cialdini's tactic of scarcity in chapter 3:

- *Scarcity*—People are more likely to do or buy something if they feel there's limited availability or opportunity.

I reserve two others for chapter 6:

- *Compliance (authority)*—People feel a sense of obligation to those in positions of authority.
- *Conformity (social proof)*—Individuals seek to be more like others they feel similar to.

I don't cover one of Cialdini's weapons in this book, but I bet you can figure out how it might apply to your product:

- *Liking*—People are more subject to influence when they like the person doing the influencing.

This chapter will also cover two other concepts relevant to influence:

- *Consultation*—People feel more invested in products on which they've provided input, or been asked to contribute feedback on the development or improvement of, than those they haven't.
- *Visual influence*—There are many design best practices and strategies for presenting users with information in a way that guides their behavior.

### 5.2.1 *Reciprocity*

*Reciprocity* is when people give or receive something with the expectation of giving or receiving something back. For example, Charu signs up for a three-month trial of Spotify's premium service for a discounted price (figure 5.2). When Charu's trial expires, she moves forward with signing up for a full-priced subscription, even though other streaming services have similar offers. Charu feels like Spotify has treated her well and given her something that has a tangible value. She also feels a sense of loyalty toward Spotify that she doesn't feel toward any of the other streaming services. Charu signing up for Spotify after the discounted trial is an example of the concept of reciprocity.

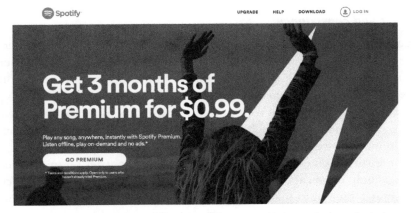

**Figure 5.2   Spotify offers users three months to use their premium product at a deep discount. This technique creates feelings of reciprocity.**

People tend to return favors, pay back debt, and treat others how they've been treated. This leads to a feeling of obligation if someone has given us concessions or discounts. We avoid feeling in debt to others when we engage in reciprocity.

Businesses engage in reciprocity when they give away free samples, coupons, discounts, or trinkets such as branded pens, USB drives, or coffee mugs to potential customers. At a higher level, businesses woo big clients with expensive gifts such as bottles of wine, tickets to sporting events, and meals at nice restaurants, in the hopes the potential client will reciprocate with a contract for business.

---

### Dear reciprocity, you suck.

Have you ever given someone you didn't really like a gift because they got you one? Or worse, have you ever gotten a gift from someone and you didn't have one to give in return? That feeling of discomfort is due to reciprocity. When you purchase a gift for someone or you pay for their lunch unexpectedly, and they say, "Oh, you shouldn't have," it's probably because you've just made them feel a sense of obligation to do something similar for you in the future—reciprocity.

Reciprocity is also why your friend comes out to pick you up when your car breaks down in the middle of nowhere at 3 a.m. Sure, they're good people, but they're also building social capital with you. If their car breaks down or they need a ride to the airport in a month, you'll be the person they'll ask.

Reciprocity is also likely a key reason we still exist. Imagine our cave-dwelling ancestors engaging in similar forms of reciprocity as we do today. Grog the cave dude might go out and gather nuts and berries for all of the other folks living in the cave that day. Later on, Grog gets drunk on elderberry wine. The next day Grog wakes up feeling sick. Instead of letting him starve to death due to a hangover, all of the other cave folk bring him back some nuts and berries to repay him for the nice deed he did the previous day.

That's a win for Grog and a win for humanity.

---

### 5.2.2   *Commitment and consistency*

People have a desire to remain consistent in their behaviors. *Commitment and consistency* is the underlying logic when people say, "My word is my bond." Your friend, for example, might agree to help you move three months before you're scheduled to move. The day before you're scheduled to move, another friend might ask this person to go to the movies on the day of your move. Your friend is more likely to decline the invitation to the movie, even though it sounds like more fun than helping you move, in order to remain consistent with the commitment he's already made to you.

Andrea regularly creates, edits, and reviews Wikipedia entries on topics she has an interest in teaching others about (figure 5.3). A Wikipedia admin notices her commitment to keeping their information accurate. The moderator reaches out and asks Andrea if she'd be willing to monitor a series of posts related to topics on which she has expertise. This would give her a more official role with Wikipedia. Andrea agrees, as the behavior of monitoring these posts is consistent with her commitment to ensuring the accuracy of Wikipedia entries.

Much like the heuristics from chapter 3, consistency allows people to reduce their mental load when making a decision. You don't need to think deeply about a decision if you already know it's consistent with previous commitments and decisions you've made.

Brands are a huge part of commitment and consistency; brand loyalty is a well-documented phenomenon. We see this reflected in the Coca Cola drinkers who'd rather drink sand than drink a Pepsi product, and the Mac users who would never dream of touching a PC operating on Windows. People are willing to pay more money to stay consistent with their commitment to a specific brand that has earned their loyalty.

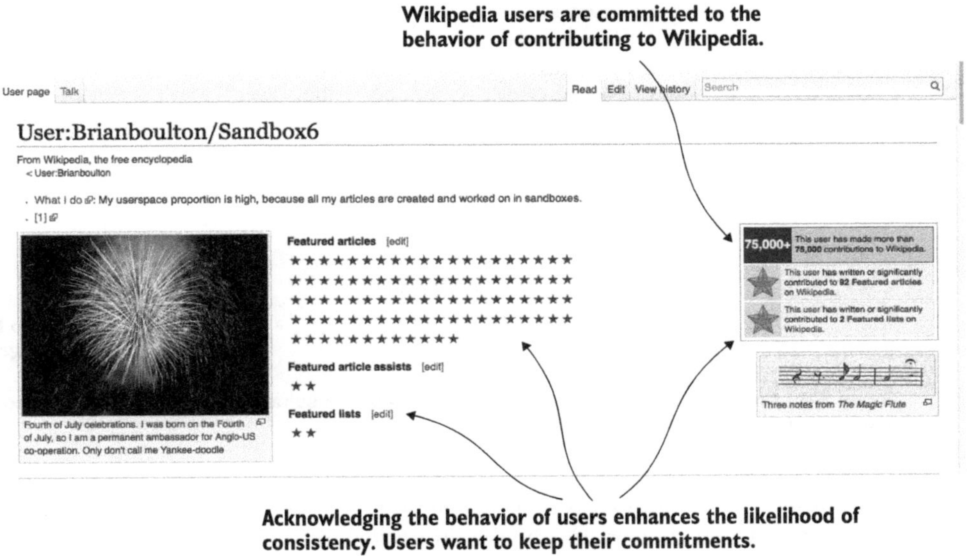

**Wikipedia users are committed to the behavior of contributing to Wikipedia.**

**Acknowledging the behavior of users enhances the likelihood of consistency. Users want to keep their commitments.**

Figure 5.3 Wikipedia benefits from having committed users help maintain information accuracy; it asks some users to take on additional obligations consistent with their previous behaviors.

### 5.2.3 Consultation

*Consultation* involves offering people an opportunity to provide input on the development of a product or service. People feel invested when they're engaged as part of a process. Consultation shows people that you value what they have to say and consider them an integral part of the decision-making process.

Ross logs onto his Chase credit card account to make a payment. He notices the icon asking for feedback (figure 5.4). Ross decides to share an idea he has for reducing the amount of steps it takes to schedule a payment in the future. A week later, Ross receives an email from a member of the Chase UX team explaining that his idea was well received and Chase will include a workflow similar to his suggestion in an upcoming update to their payment portal. Ross is thrilled and feels a deeper commitment to using his Chase card over other credit cards he actively maintains.

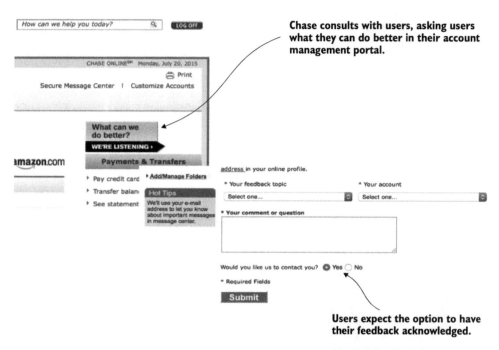

**Figure 5.4    Chase gives users an opportunity to provide consultation directly from their account management portal.**

Committees are another form of consultation. Leaders of organizations often form committees when they want to make an important decision. Even if the organization won't end up taking the committee's advice, the act of forming the committee and allowing the committee to work with other members of the organization is a sign that leadership sought consultation. This can lead to increased buy-in from members.

### 5.2.4    *Visual influence*

*Visual influence* involves techniques used to meaningfully display information to people—to get them to immediately pay attention to the important things you're presenting. People interpret colors, signs, symbols, and sounds in ways that influence behaviors.

Ezekiel is about to pick up his friends to play basketball. He decides to check the weather before leaving his house. He looks on the weather service website and sees the image in figure 5.5. Ezekiel doesn't bother to read the actual forecast—he's seen enough. Instead of picking up his friends, Ezekiel hides in his basement the rest of the day. Ezekiel has been influenced by the visual displayed on the weather service's website.

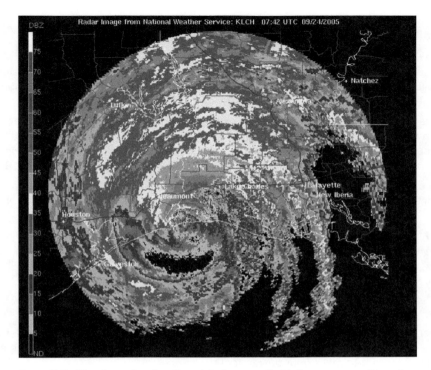

**Figure 5.5  Weather radar visualizes data in a way that influences users through both color and shape.**

Visual influence is different across settings and can include the size and color of words and pictures, the order of items in lists (people pay more attention to what comes first in a list), and where you locate items on a screen (for example, the left side is where most people look first).

## 5.3  *How to design for influence*

We're in a unique position to influence our users with digital design. No other medium can provide the depth and breadth of information as quickly as digital designs can. We can reach our users in almost any context, providing them with enhanced experiences and opportunities for engagement with our product. I believe influence is inherent to our design—we'll influence our potential users and users regardless; we need to use influence thoughtfully.

**A voice from the past: How to be more like Dale Carnegie**

Dale Carnegie is what most people would consider a badass dude. He came from an impoverished family in Missouri to start one of the most recognizable professional development, sales, and public speaking training services in the world. His motivational speaking engagements consistently filled large venues.

Carnegie believed the best approach to influencing people was not to attempt to get them to listen to your great ideas, but to actually shut up and listen and learn about the person you want to influence. He put these ideas into a book, *How to Make Friends and Influence People*, that has sold millions of copies since being published in 1936.

Carnegie puts forth the following key ideas for influencing others in a section of the book focusing on how to get people to like you (a key step if you want to influence folks):

1   Become genuinely interested in other people.
2   Smile.
3   Remember that a person's name is to that person the sweetest sound in any language.
4   Be a good listener. Encourage others to talk about themselves.
5   Talk in terms of the other person's interest.
6   Make the person feel important—and do it sincerely.

I strongly recommend you pick up a copy of Mr. Carnegie's book and learn the details of his strategy to influence people. You'll find much of it relevant to your daily life and to how you want to make your design feel to users.

### 5.3.1   *Creating a sense of reciprocity*

You design for reciprocity when you make users feel a sense of obligation toward use of your product.

Tia is looking online for a handy guide on Adobe Photoshop keyboard shortcuts. She finds Noble Desktop's free guide offered on their website. She bookmarks the Keyboard Shortcuts Guides page (figure 5.6) and comes back later for additional Adobe product cheat sheets. Later, Tia uses her professional development funds to take the Noble Desktop course on Advanced Retouching in Photoshop. She doesn't think twice about shopping around for another course provider. Tia was motivated to take a paid course from Noble by the feeling of reciprocity elicited from the free content she initially accessed.

Offering useful free material increases the likelihood of appeal to users.

More freebies = more reciprocity.

Noble offers free "Goodies," creating a sense of reciprocity in users.

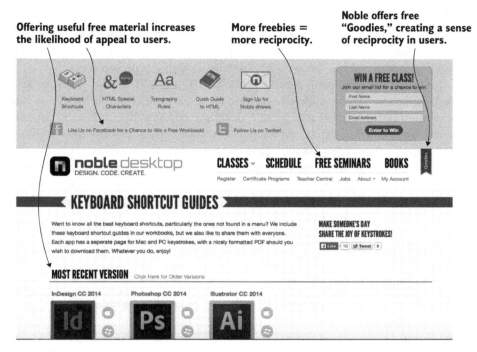

**Figure 5.6** Offering free content that's useful is a way to generate goodwill and reciprocity from users.

### HOW TO DESIGN FOR RECIPROCITY

You use reciprocity as a negotiation tactic with your users. As such, you need to remember two things are key for successful reciprocity:

- You need to give your users something.
- You need to ask your users for something.

You should identify what you have that might be enticing to users. You can

- Share knowledge based on your experiences by offering white papers or cheat sheets for your industry.
- Offer free content in the form of guides, templates, and research findings.
- Offer product discounts or coupons for free shipping, if applicable.

In return, you should ask users to provide information for you to learn more about them and to contact them in the future. You can capture users' email addresses and demographic information to help facilitate follow-up marketing of your product, or even to inform your design of your product. Wouldn't it be interesting to find a majority of users signing up for your sex tips white paper are over the age of 70?

If you plan for users to engage in social networking through your product, you also need to design for reciprocity between users. Provide users with an opportunity to exchange ideas or information that facilitates a sense of reciprocity toward each other. Doing so will increase the social ties users create through your product.

## 5.3.2   *Activating commitment and consistency*

You create commitment and consistency when you show users how use of your product is in line with their beliefs. Commitment and consistency manifests itself as customer loyalty in the way we see Mac users using only Apple products.

Juanita has been using Adobe products (figure 5.7) for her creative and design needs since she was in high school. She feels a strong sense of loyalty to Adobe and recommends their products to her designer friends. She has also contributed to forums on how to use advanced features on Adobe programs she uses regularly. Using anything else just feels wrong. Juanita immediately downloads newly released or updated Adobe products without question, demonstrating commitment and consistency in her behavior. She's also displaying behavior consistent with the escalation of commitment heuristic (section 3.3.6), in which she's avoiding the cost of learning new software from another company.

**Adobe offers users a variety of products in the hopes that committing to use one leads to consistency of choosing other Adobe products over the competition.**

**Creative Suites makes it easy for users to practice consistency in their commitment to using Adobe products across tasks.**

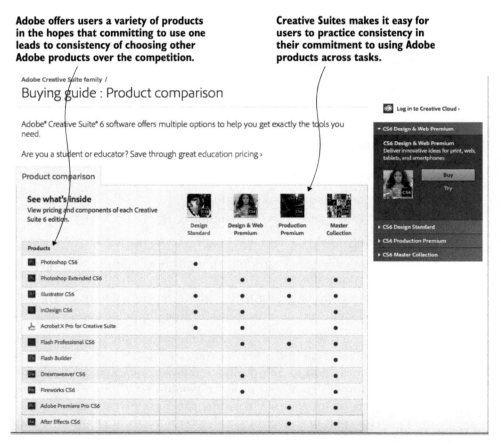

**Figure 5.7   Adobe provides individual products as well as packages, with the hopes you'll remain committed and consistently use additional products or one of its product suites.**

### HOW TO DESIGN FOR COMMITMENT AND CONSISTENCY

You can work with your marketing and communications team to answer such questions as: What commitment can you get users to make? How can you capitalize on consistency with your loyal users? Most products will have many options. Examples of commitment you can incorporate into your experience include

- *Creating a profile in your system*—The effort users put forth creating a profile will reflect a commitment they've made to use your product. You can encourage profile completion in a way similar to LinkedIn.
- *Make commitments public*—Online petitions, posts on social media, reviews, and message board discussions all can reflect a public commitment to your product. You should look to make these spaces available to facilitate this activity wherever it makes sense.
- *Offering a smaller sale that builds into a bigger sale or commitment*—Do you have the availability to offer smaller pieces of your product at a reduced cost? If you offer a suite of products, such as Adobe with their Creative Suite, can you offer users a discount if they purchase one product and then want to try others?
- *Building on existing commitments*—Many of your users are already engaged in a number of commitments that can help your cause. If you're designing an iOS application, how can you tap into your target users' commitment to the "Cult of Mac"? Can you offer your product as an add-on "No iPhone users should go without?" If you provide financial management software, you can target users of your monthly budgeting software to stay consistent and use your tax preparation software. This is what brand loyalty is all about.

## 5.3.3 *Facilitating consultation*

You address consultation when you incorporate the voice of users and potential users in your process. Effective consultation involves more than asking for feedback; you need to show users that you've incorporated the feedback as well. Or you can provide reasons you won't reflect feedback in your design if it doesn't make sense.

Reuben is part of a group of users asked to beta test a new iOS calendar and reminder application. The app's designers have asked the beta testers to use the app for a month and report on any bugs as well as any issues with usability. Three months later, the app is released to the public. Reuben, along with 80% of the individuals involved in beta testing the app, pay to have access to the public release. Reuben feels invested in the success of the app, and immediately changes his behavior to using the app as his primary calendar-keeping tool. He also recommends the app to other users and writes a 5-star review on the App Store. The app's design team created buy-in from Reuben and the other beta testers through the concept of consultation, making them part of the process.

### HOW TO DESIGN FOR CONSULTATION

You can build goodwill and gain insight with users and potential users through effective use of consultation. Beta testing, inviting users to a special preview or to be early adopters (and provide feedback), and creating user advisory groups are good methods of facilitating user consolation of your product.

If you work as a consultant, you should also realize that you have an incredible responsibility for influencing the design of your client's product. Actively seek your client's input and feedback as you design using a variety of the previous methods.

The Disability Rights Fund, an international organization leading the advocacy for the rights of disabled persons, recommends consultancy as a critical component of a strategy to facilitate participation, engagement, and inclusion. They recommend a number of relevant tips for organizing your consultation efforts (see the additional resources for the URL):

- *Clarify your objectives*—Don't promise more than you're able or willing to do with the information you're requesting.
- *Create alliances*—You want to ensure you have allies and not just people giving you advice. Trust and commitment to shared goals is an important part of an alliance.
- *Collect information from diverse groups*—If you allow only one type of user to form your design decisions, you're leaving out the potential for diverse opinions and unique ideas from a large number of potential users. Identify key stakeholder groups and seek consultation from representatives from multiple groups.
- *Report your findings*—Your users want to know what you do with their feedback. I see organizations frequently fail to report what they've found when conducting research or consulting with their users or constituents. People who agree to participate in studies or serve on committees have a stake in knowing the outcome of their work. If you create a document based on your findings, you should share it publicly. If you've made decisions based on consultation with your stakeholders, you should credit them in your press releases and on your product's website. If you decide not to take the advice of your stakeholders, that's okay—you should still acknowledge their efforts and provide some insight into the thought process that led to your decision.

### 5.3.4  *Visual influence*

Digital design teams are uniquely positioned to visually influence users. Visual influence and appeal is critical for design. Yes, we all say we've moved beyond just making our websites or applications look pretty. But if we make our supremely usable experiences ugly, they'll be unused. And pretty can add to functionality. Visual and graphic design is an active field of study. There are a number of books and resources for influencing viewers through visual design, some of which I list in the additional resources section. There might be limitless potential guidance on visual design, but here are 10 best practices for influencing using visual design you should always think about:

- Use visuals and images to provide context and enhance the meaning of the text.
- Use high-contrast colors for visual information and the background.
- Don't overwhelm a page with content.
- Draw attention visually to critical content.
- Use familiar icons wherever possible.
- Let typography be your friend.
- Have content unfold in the order it should be read.

- Draw viewers in with human faces.
- Put objects that are related closer together.
- Keep in mind color blindness and issues of accessibility.

You can use these 10 guidelines to ensure you're accounting for visual influence with your design. Keep issues related to accessibility in mind when you focus on your visual design. Many users are color blind, have low vision, or are blind; these users don't benefit as much from visual appeal as they do from great functionality. You can balance a visually appealing product with accessibility to create the ultimate influential experience. Make sure your design is screen reader–friendly.

There are no limits to the types of visual influence your design can convey. I'll provide examples of four themes visual design can convey:

- Creativity
- Leadership
- Power
- Professionalism

### CREATIVITY

Intuitive Company's blog (figure 5.8) shows the world what we do during our day jobs and beyond, creating a personal connection with users and highlighting our creativity.

**Figure 5.8  The homepage of Intuitive Company's blog highlights the conferences staff members attend and make presentations, awards their designs have won, thought pieces, and human interest stories that inspire creativity.**

You can design to reflect the creativity of your product and team. People enjoy seeing the human side; showing your users biographical information and stories about the lives of your staff can go a long way toward humanizing your product and making users aware of the creative forces on your team.

### LEADERSHIP

Apple demonstrates their leadership through the refined look of their homepage (figure 5.9). They don't beat users over the head with images and text; they let their simplicity and branding do the talking. They also focus on pictures of their product—the product that has made them leaders in tech.

Your logo, the font you use, and the content you display all contribute to how users perceive you as a leader in your field. You can have a great product that solves the problem at hand, but if you display something similar to the car wash example later in this chapter (see figure 5.11), users won't take you seriously.

**Apple knows users view them and their products as leaders in the field. The visual highlighting of their product is also a visual display of leadership. Simple and effective.**

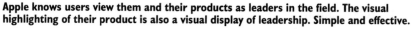

iPad Air 2
Change is in the Air.

**Figure 5.9   Apple's product design is reflective of its leadership in tech.**

### POWER

Audi conveys the power of their product and their brand through the use of space and focus on the product image, and by contrasting black text on white background (figure 5.10). Their website makes you want to climb into your monitor and take their cars for a spin.

Your design conveys power when you focus on simplicity and trust. Highlight your product in a way that visually sets it apart from the competition. Don't use an abundance of superlatives in describing your product. You shouldn't say, "The greatest thing since sliced bread!" unless you can say "Bread Times Magazine rated us the greatest thing since sliced bread!"

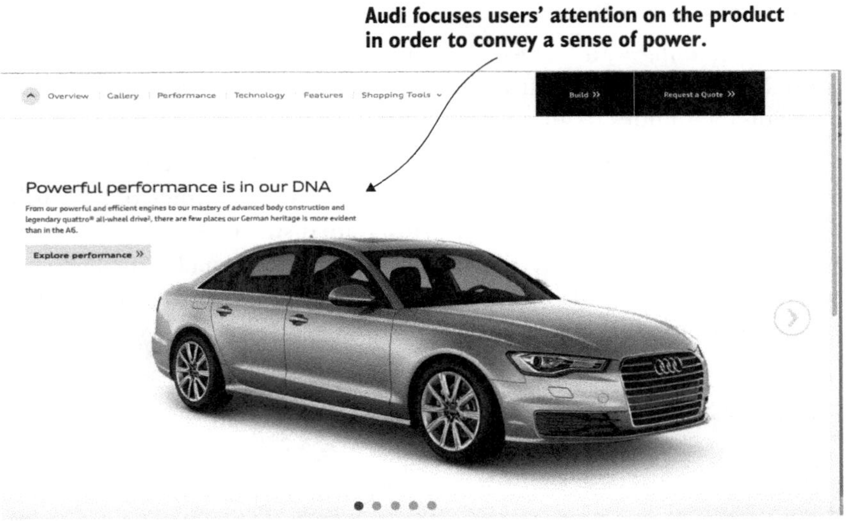

**Audi focuses users' attention on the product in order to convey a sense of power.**

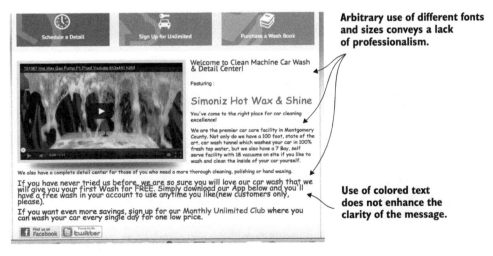

**Figure 5.10** **Audi conveys power through the simplicity of its design and the focus of the page on one large image of their product.**

### PROFESSIONALISM

Figure 5.11 shows a local car wash's website. The distracting and outdated layout, mixed use of font sizes and colored text, and unclear label on the video cause users concern that this lack of professionalism extends beyond the website to the business itself.

Your website or application conveys professionalism, regardless of the topic, by adhering to the conventions of visual design covered in this section.

**Arbitrary use of different fonts and sizes conveys a lack of professionalism.**

**Use of colored text does not enhance the clarity of the message.**

**Figure 5.11** **Sure, it's a car wash. Don't invest in having a website that might be doing a better job for your competition.**

### 5.3.5   *Influence to stay away from*

People consider *influence* a bad word because many have gone before us and screwed things up. Many designs are still screwing things up. I don't recommend using any of the following techniques to attempt to influence your users.

#### THE "MAKE SOMEONE FEEL DUMB FOR NOT USING YOUR PRODUCT" POP-UP INFLUENCE

CNBC and Car and Driver (figures 5.12 and 5.13) are examples of sites using a technique I'm finding to be more common, and quite disturbing: providing sarcastic statements users need to click on to avoid joining their email list. These statements attempt to influence users through a fear of loss—they'll lose out on valuable information and opportunities if they don't sign up.

Belittling users won't make them more likely to use your product. Everyone needs the "most important news."

**Figure 5.12   Hey CNBC, everyone needs the most important news.**

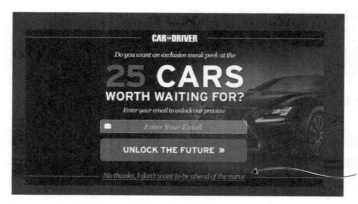

No one is unlocking the future by giving you their email address. Don't make users feel bad because they choose not to give you information.

**Figure 5.13   Oh, *Car and Driver*. If only I signed up for your sneak peek, I'd have been so ahead of the curve!**

Don't belittle users for choosing not to provide you with information. I advocate treating users with respect at all times in the usability and usefulness of your design, as well as the content you present them.

### THE "SHOW AS MANY STOCK PHOTOS REPRESENTING WEALTH AS YOU CAN" WEBSITE

Somehow, get-rich-quick schemes go hand in hand with the internet. I think this is just a modern version of triangle schemes, telling people they can get rich quick by stuffing envelopes. I don't plan to find out, because I'm positive a reputable site that would offer a product where users make money wouldn't have a design that includes clip art pictures of piles of gold coins (figure 5.14). You can be confident any design involving pictures like these is not a good idea.

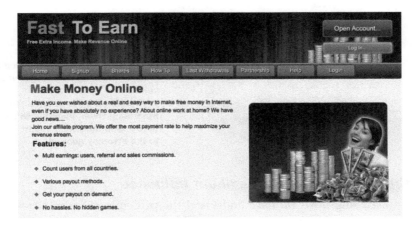

**Figure 5.14  Fast to Earn makes me feel fast to click another site.**

### CALLING YOUR PRODUCT A MIRACLE

Miracle Shake plays off people's hopes for an easy cure to a difficult problem. They highlight that pharmaceutical companies are threatening them with a lawsuit. Figure 5.15 is an attempt to convince users their product is so successful that it's competing with the pharmaceutical industry.

Making impossible-to-keep promises or claims is sure to turn users against you once they try your product. Even if

**Figure 5.15  Yes, people are still selling snake oil. Diabetesfree.org proves this point.**

your product is a miracle, you should find other ways to say it. The example in figure 5.15 attempts to influence users by calling their product a miracle, as well as by highlighting the threats they face, suggesting that others feel threatened by how great their product is. Diabetesfree.org also prevents users from leaving the site when first attempting to close the tab (figure 5.16).

Figure 5.16   Never use a dialog box to block users from leaving your page unless they'll lose valuable information they've entered. You risk frustrating them. I wanted to click a third option that would report the site to the attorney general.

## 5.4   *Talking the talk: Conversations about influence*

You'll enjoy discussing how you have addressed the principle of influence with your clients. Here are some examples of how you might approach the topics covered in this chapter:

- *Reciprocity*—"We're making a number of white papers and articles your staff has written on relevant topics available for free access to users in our newly designed 'Content and Tools Center.' Providing this value-added experience will enhance your current users' loyalty and create a sense of connection with your product in potential users."

- *Commitment and consistency*—"We're holding a contest where users of your current product can tweet how they use it and why they like it. Three users will receive your newly released product for free. We'll display the tweets on a promotional page on your product's website, as well as retweet many of them. This public display of affection toward your product generates a sense of loyalty in users as well as makes it more likely they'll identify with your other products to meet their needs."

- *Consultation*—"We've created a timeline for creating opportunities for users to provide feedback on your product. We want to create a user advisory group to test your updated products, give these users access to early versions of your product, and ask them to spread the word about your product and the value it provides."

- *Visual influence*—"We interviewed users and found that they identify your brand with security and trust. We highlight these traits in the simplicity of our design and the content we associate with your brand, and by displaying the industry safety awards you've received throughout the pages of your product's website. We've also designed the application to address many of the issues with visually locating information we found several users struggled with during usability testing."

## 5.5　*Case study: LinkedIn*

LinkedIn is one of the largest social networking services in existence, focusing mainly on professional networking and knowledge sharing. According to LinkedIn's About Us page, they started in Reid Hoffman's living room in 2002, and now exist as a community of over 300 million users in 200 countries and territories. LinkedIn thrives on many concepts of the principle of influence. LinkedIn provides users with the ability to gain influence with each other, use influence on each other, and influence potential employers.

### 5.5.1　*Reciprocity*

Individuals engage in a number of acts that lead to reciprocity (figure 5.17), including

- Liking, sharing, and commenting on posts
- Endorsing skills and expertise
- Providing testimonials

**Endorsing others creates reciprocity among LinkedIn users, thereby increasing their use and the usefulness of LinkedIn.**

**Figure 5.17　LinkedIn fosters reciprocity when asking users to endorse other users' skills and expertise.**

### 5.5.2  *Commitment and consistency*

LinkedIn creates an environment that facilitates commitment and consistency from users. Building a profile in LinkedIn is a time-consuming task. Users don't want to waste their time, so once they've built a profile it's more likely they'll keep it up to date. A LinkedIn profile serves as a living document recording users' professional accomplishments—this means users will want to consistently update their profile as they achieve milestones.

LinkedIn also fosters commitment, allowing users to log in to other sites (for example, Bloomberg Careers, figure 5.18) through their LinkedIn profile credentials. Users logging in through their LinkedIn profile have created a deeper commitment to LinkedIn as it now serves as their means for accessing additional content through other products.

**Bloomberg Careers, like many other sites, allows users to log in with their LinkedIn credentials. This creates consistency and commitment in LinkedIn user's behaviors.**

Figure 5.18   Bloomberg Careers is one of many sites that allows users to log in using LinkedIn. This fosters LinkedIn users' feelings of commitment and consistency with using LinkedIn.

### 5.5.3  *Consultation*

LinkedIn also engages in a traditional form of consultation, asking for user feedback (figure 5.19). Unfortunately, LinkedIn makes it clear they won't respond to users who provide feedback. I wouldn't recommend this approach. I don't think LinkedIn needs to respond to every suggestion they receive, but I think they should leave open the possibility with a less abrasive disclaimer such as "We appreciate all feedback we receive. We are not able to reply to every submission, but we do consider all feedback."

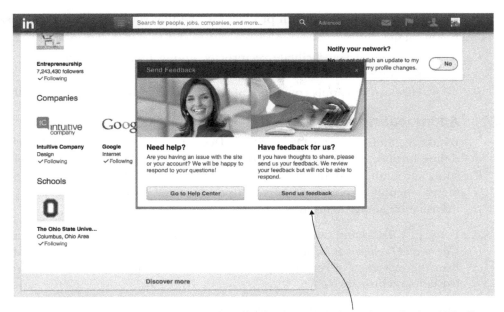

**Soliciting feedback is an excellent form of consultation. LinkedIn defeats the purpose when they inform users they will not respond.**

**Figure 5.19   Soliciting feedback is a traditional form of consultation—although I'm not impressed that LinkedIn states it won't respond to feedback.**

## 5.6   *End-of-chapter exercise: Applying the principle of influence*

Francine has just received funding for "Tech and Stained Glass Daily," her startup idea that combines a website and an application to deliver up-to-the-minute news and analysis on tech trends—specifically focusing on those related to the art of stained glass. Francine faces a number of barriers to entry in the cutthroat world of tech and stained glass news. She needs to influence potential users to try her product. Use ideas from this chapter to complete the following exercises. You can share your answers and provide feedback on the Manning Publications forum here: https://forums.manning .com/forums/design-for-the-mind.

- How might Francine use reciprocity to influence users to try her product?
- What type of consultation could Francine seek from potential users?
- Where and how would she locate potential users of her product?
- Use the space below to sketch a visual design of Francine's homepage that would convey elements of visual influence I covered in this chapter.

Now, thinking about your own product, or one that you're familiar with, answer the following questions:

- How might you facilitate reciprocity among users or potential users of your product?
- How can you apply commitment and consistency to users of your product?

## 5.7    *Additional resources*

Barak, A., and O. Gluck-Ofri. (2007). Degree and reciprocity of self-disclosure in online forums. *CyberPsychology & Behavior*, 10(3), 407–417. (Researchers conducted a study and found evidence to support reciprocity of self-disclosure in online environments—people respond to others that post personal information by posting personal information about themselves.)

Berg, J., J. Dickhaut, and K. McCabe. (1995). Trust, reciprocity, and social history. *Games and Economic Behavior*, 10(1), 122–142. (Researchers conducted a study to confirm the existence of reciprocity, and show that having a social history strengthens trust and reciprocity.)

Cialdini, R.B. (2001). *Influence: Science and practice* (4th ed.). Boston: Allyn & Bacon. (Cialdini's seminal work defining his weapons of influence)

Dellarocas, C., M. Fan, and C.A. Wood. (2004). Self-interest, reciprocity, and participation in online reputation systems. MIT Center for Digital Business, Cambridge, MA. Available at http://bit.ly/1pILkqh. (Researchers demonstrated that people leaving feedback on eBay purchasing experiences are often motivated by self-interest. People expect reciprocity in the form of feedback from others when they leave feedback.)

Disability Rights Fund. (ND). Good practice: Consultation process. Available at www.disabilityrightsfund.org/resource/good-practice-consultation-process.html. (The Disability Rights Fund provides a valuable how-to guide for engaging in consultation.)

Sherwin, K. (2015). Low-contrast text is not the answer. Nielsen Norman Group. Available at www.nngroup.com/articles/low-contrast/. (Nielson Norman Group researchers provide guidance on enhancing visual design without decreasing usability.)

KEYWORDS: consistency and commitment, consultation, influence, reciprocity, visual influence

## 5.8    *Summary*

- Elements of influence have an effect on individuals' attitudes and behaviors toward your product.
- We want to positively influence users' attitudes toward use of our product.
- Reciprocity is the act of influencing a person through creating a sense of obligation; we achieve this by giving away content, providing free and deeply

discounted trials, and offering opportunities for users to engage in liking or sharing others' work through our platform.

- Commitment and consistency reflect the fact that individuals want their behaviors to be consistent with commitments and with past behaviors.
- Consultation involves giving users and potential users a voice during the design process. Steering committees, beta testers, usability testing, user interviews, and other methods of making users feel they've contributed to your product are ways to address consultation.
- Visual influence requires an understanding of your product and what traits (for example, thoughtful or creative) you want users to assign to your product. You'll need to test your design to ensure you're effective at visually conveying the influence you want to have on users.

# Using family, friends, and social networks to influence users

6

**This chapter covers**

- Understanding the influence of family, friends, and social networks on your users
- Ensuring your design accommodates social influence
- Identifying areas for design improvement to address social influence
- Discussing social influence with others
- Applying the principles of social influence in digital design contexts

Kara is an interaction designer new to Philadelphia. She took a job working at a local design firm. She considers herself a designer who is a foodie, history lover, and fan of independent films. Knowing this about herself helps her find others in the Philadelphia area with similar interests. Kara meets a number of other designers with similar interests and some who are the opposite of her—they have no interest in food, history, and independent films (*social comparison*).

Kara finds out from the designers she identifies with that many of them are joining a Slack.com group set up for designers in the Philadelphia area. Kara has never used Slack, but she requests access to the group once one of her new design colleagues suggests she does (*compliance*). She then sees that many of the people she associates with are signing up for the "local events" channel within the Slack group.

Kara registers for and attends a local event that'll include a national speaker many of her design colleagues regard as a leader in the field. The speaker recommends a new tool interaction designers might find useful. Based on this advice, Kara downloads this tool when she goes back home.

Kara's social network has influenced many of her decisions. The web is a social place. You're probably well aware of this. Statistically, you're probably engaging in at least one type of social interaction online on a regular basis—even if you're only a consumer of information. According to Pew Research Center (http://mng.bz/ 2KM6), in 2014 over 70% of U.S. internet users were on Facebook, and over 50% of U.S. adults use two or more forms of online social media. We see this growth reflected in companies bombarding us with messages and advertisements over our social media feeds. These companies want to reach people, and they know people are using social media.

Users and potential users of our products don't just hang out on social media all day. Users are exploring other social areas of the web, such as blogging, reading and writing product reviews, rating applications, and sharing content they find interesting. Researchers have explored the impact and influence others have on our decisions and behaviors. This chapter focuses on how your design can harness the power of social influence and social identity (figure 6.1) to use the web and other digital channels to increase awareness and use of your product.

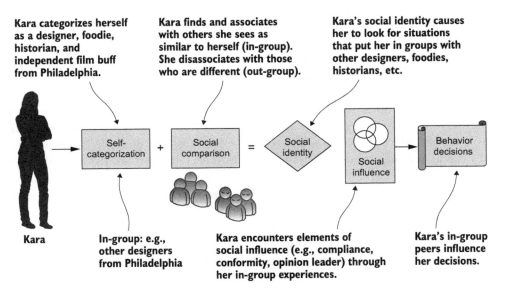

**Figure 6.1** Individuals develop a social identity through self-categorization and social comparison. Social influence encompasses influence techniques involving other individuals and groups.

## 6.1     Introduction

Humans are naturally social; it's how we've survived. We need to develop identities that allow us to relate to others. This chapter will cover how your design can use websites and mobile devices as platforms for delivering designs that make the most of social influence. We know word of mouth is one of the best ways to convince others to try our product. People trust the recommendations of friends and family. We also know that others are more likely to purchase products with positive reviews. You'll learn more in this chapter about how we can harness the power of these types of interactions.

> **NOTE**  Social influence complements chapter 2's planned behavior and chapter 3's decisions under risk. Your users' behavioral choices are heavily influenced by their social identity. Your design incorporates the power of groups and people your users relate to when you account for social influence.

### 6.1.1     Brief academic background

Social Identity Theory provides the foundation for some of what we'll cover in this chapter. Social Identity Theory was born in Britain from the work of Bristol University professor Henri Tajfel and his colleague John Turner. Tajfel's past strongly influenced his research agenda. He was a soldier who fought against the Germans in World War II and spent time as a prisoner of war, which led to his curiosity in what caused people to engage in groupthink and mistreatment of members of other groups. He was interested in understanding how something as terrible as the Holocaust could happen. His research goal was to identify the conditions that would lead members of one group to discriminate against members of another group. In 1979, Tajfel and Turner published a chapter (see the additional resources) arguing that there are many situations in life in which an individual doesn't act as an individual but as a member of a group they identify with.

Tajfel and Turner conducted a number of experiments in which they found that the simple act of belonging to a group increased the likelihood of discrimination. The researchers conducted experiments where they randomly assigned people to various fictitious groups. They asked the individuals in each group to allocate a scarce resource (such as money) to other people. The research participants consistently allotted more of whatever the resource was to others identified as being part of the same fictitious group researchers had assigned them to. Researchers also found that people asked to rate the members of their fictitious group consistently rated members they were told had "migrated" from another group as less favorable than group members that hadn't. The researchers concluded that something as small as belonging to a fictitious group led to an increase in discrimination against out-group members.

Researchers have also examined why people choose not to conform, or diverge, from what others are doing. People who don't conform to groupthink do so for a number of reasons: They don't identify with the group making the decisions. They identify more strongly with another, more influential group. They identify with a strong opinion leader with a diverging opinion. Researchers have often found that surveillance, or publicly stating an opinion, increases conformity. People are more likely to conform to an opinion or a behavior if they know what they think or do will be public. People are less likely to conform when they're able to state an opinion or engage in a behavior privately.

Social Identity Theory gives us insight into the formation and behavior of groups online as well as off. Researchers have used this theory to help understand the behavior of online health communities and online gaming communities and the exchange of information and ideas between individuals online. Researchers consistently find that the social groups people identify with or wish to belong to influence their attitudes and behaviors.

## 6.2   *Key concepts of social influence*

Researchers have identified many factors related to social influence that are relevant to your design. We'll cover Social Identity Theory, social validation and likability, compliance, conformity, and opinion leaders in this chapter.

### 6.2.1   *Social Identity Theory*

We each develop identities defined by the social groups in which we're members. For example, many people are members of religious groups, political groups, sports teams, university alumni groups, professional organizations, and hobby groups. These groups help us define who we are (our social identity) and often shape our decisions. Note that you can be a member of more than one of these groups, so context counts in determining which group you identify with the most at any given time.

We also seek to distance ourselves from those we feel are unlike our own group. Each example I gave earlier has an opposing or at least different group: incompatible religions, political opposites, fans of rival sports teams, alumni of other universities, members of different professional organizations or different professions, and those not involved in similar causes or interests we hold.

Social Identity Theory describes how people develop their social identities and why this is important in decision-making. Tajfel and Turner identified two key processes individuals engage in to develop their social identities:

- *Self-categorization*—Individuals assign themselves to categories based on their perception of how their attitudes, beliefs, and behaviors align with these categories.
- *Social comparison*—Individuals compare themselves to others and then label their traits as alike (in-group) or unalike (out-group).

Tajfel and Turner suggest people initially go through the process of self-categorization. They categorize themselves based on many interests or traits, including music interests, religion, technology preferences, whether they drink Coke or Pepsi, and an infinite number of other possible categories. If Kara is going through self-categorization, she might categorize herself as a heavy metal–loving, craft beer–drinking, Apple user.

Next, she'll engage in social comparison. Kara will look around to see who's similar to her and who's different, and align herself with groups of similar-minded people.

She'll look for fans of similar music. Maybe she'll join a Meetup that focuses on heavy metal. She'll look for opportunities to engage in activities with other craft beer lovers, say by joining a "craft beer of the month" club. To top it all off, she might create a local organization dedicated to drinking craft beer while discussing the latest Mac products.

Kara might check Meetup.com (figure 6.2) to decide what to do on a Saturday night based on what her heavy metal friends are interested in doing. And she might sample new brews recommended by her craft beer buddies, while avoiding ones ranked as unpalatable by members of the group.

Kara will also look to create distance between her and other unsimilar groups. She might avoid wearing similar clothing as members of a group with different musical interests. She wouldn't want to drink wine in order to avoid classification as a wine lover, and she certainly wouldn't be caught using a Microsoft product. Kara can become more like her in-group members by becoming less like her out-group members. These traits will also serve as cues to whom she might want to spend more or less time with. Yes, judging a book by its cover is part of social identity.

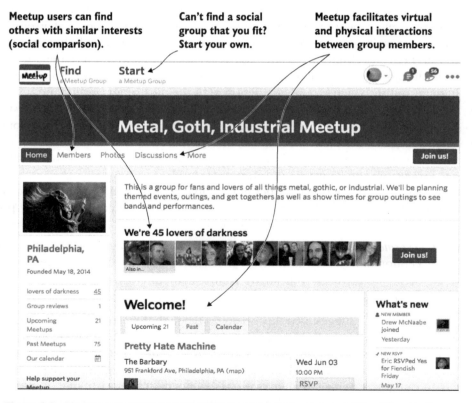

Figure 6.2    Meetup.com exists to help fulfill our desire to develop social identities. To those about to rock, I salute you.

### 6.2.2    *Social validation*

Arlene is a new mom and has just returned to work after having her child. She isn't satisfied with the look and size of the bag she's using to carry her breast pump and supplies to work. Arlene posts a comment on a message board for working moms on the What to Expect When You Are Expecting website (figure 6.3). She knows she shares a number of common characteristics and interests as the other women participating on the message board—she looks at them as her trusted advisers. Arlene is looking for a product using social validation from others whose opinions she trusts.

*Social validation* is the act of an individual looking at what others they view as members of their social group recommend or dislike; people consciously and unconsciously look to their peers for guidance and affirmation. Yelp is the go-to source for many individuals considering where to have dinner, particularly if they're in an unfamiliar area. Why? Because other users have socially validated highly rated Yelp restaurants, and low-rated restaurants have been socially invalidated. TripAdvisor is another example of a site many users look at for socially validated activities to do during a vacation.

Individuals engage in a number of behaviors seeking social validation as well. These include submitting work for an award, hoping for public praise on a job well done, posting on Facebook or Twitter and hoping for as many Likes or retweets as possible, and writing reviews for sites like Yelp. Reviewing a product validates it if it's positively reviewed by a member of social group.

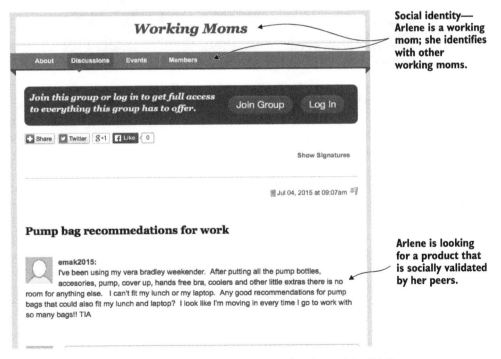

**Figure 6.3    Topical forums dedicated to specific groups allow for social validation.**

### 6.2.3   *Compliance*

Martin is 19 years old and looking for more information on local beers. He navigates to the Dogfish Head Brewery website to see which seasonal beers they're brewing. Martin immediately encounters a modal warning him that all visitors need to be 21 and asking him to enter his date of birth. Although no one is around to force him to be honest, Martin enters his correct birthday because he believes that's what he should do. He then receives a message informing him he isn't old enough to enter the website (figure 6.4). Martin demonstrated compliance with Dogfish Head's request that he enter his correct birthday.

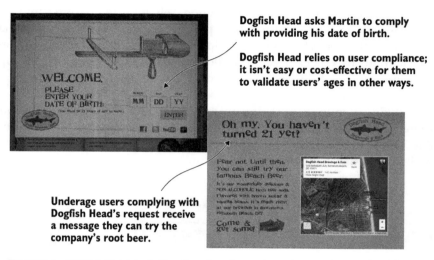

Dogfish Head asks Martin to comply with providing his date of birth.

Dogfish Head relies on user compliance; it isn't easy or cost-effective for them to validate users' ages in other ways.

Underage users complying with Dogfish Head's request receive a message they can try the company's root beer.

Figure 6.4   Dogfish Head and other American breweries ask users to comply with a request for verifying users' ages prior to granting them access to their website.

*Compliance* is when people agree to do something they're asked to do, because they realize the person or persons asking them have an expectation that they'll engage in the behavior. Often, people in authority can gain compliance from others. Decision makers must accurately interpret the desires of those making the order for compliance to effectively make their decision. You can't comply correctly with something you don't understand correctly.

Peer pressure to consume drugs or alcohol is a negative example of compliance. Someone taking time for daily exercise because their friends ask them to meet at the gym is a positive example of compliance. One key piece to compliance is that you actually ask someone to engage in the task; compliance doesn't rely on passive attempts to influence behavior.

### 6.2.4   *Conformity*

Ron uses iTunes to buy a new album his favorite band has just released. Once he has completed the purchase, iTunes surfaces recommendations based on what other users who purchased that album have bought (figure 6.5). Ron understands these must be artists people like him find enjoyable. Ron explores some of these bands and decides to purchase some of the songs recommended. Apple has influenced social conformity in Ron's behavior.

**Figure 6.5** **Apple uses conformity to encourage additional purchases on iTunes when they show users what others have bought.**

Individuals engage in *conformity* when they do something based on the norms they perceive their group or society to hold. Unlike compliance, these norms are often unstated. Individuals assume this is how they should act. For example, most people don't need to be told they shouldn't eat a sandwich while using the toilet. This is something they assume based on observation over the course of their life. When entering a brand-new situation—say, going to an art museum for the first time—most individuals will see how others are behaving and then model their behavior after what they see.

Conformity is extremely powerful in that it can prevent people from engaging in behaviors perceived to be against the norm, and it can promote individuals engaging in certain behaviors without much (or any) additional effort.

### 6.2.5   *Opinion leaders*

Ruby is a freelance designer. She follows the Twitter accounts of other designers she believes set the trend in her field. When these designers offer opinions about the latest techniques or tactics, Ruby will often apply these to her work with her clients. These *opinion leaders* influence Ruby's actions.

Opinion leaders are the people we think of and look to as being influential and wise in their decisions related to their field of expertise. There are different and many opinion leaders for each topic. World leaders might consider the President of the United States (POTUS) an opinion leader among heads of state in politics, but parent teacher organization (PTO) leaders might consider Dorothy Smith, the mother of three grade-school children down the street, as an opinion leader among local leaders. Catholics might consider the Pope as an opinion leader on Catholicism internationally, but they might consider their Bible study teacher the opinion leader on local issues related to Catholics.

Opinion leaders are critical in spreading information and awareness of a product. People look to opinion leaders to inform their decisions. If the U.S. President says world leaders need to address a specific issue, they'll begin to look closer at how they can address this issue. If Oprah Winfrey (figure 6.6) says a book she enjoyed is worth buying, many people will flock to purchase or check out the book to read. Opinion leaders play a key role influencing the groups they identify with.

**IDENTIFYING OPINION LEADERS**

You might not have an awareness of who the opinion leaders are who use your design. Here are five methods commonly used to identify opinion leaders:

**Figure 6.6    Opinion leader and kingmaker Oprah Winfrey; she's probably not reviewing my book anytime soon, but it can't hurt to hope!**

- *Celebrities*—Who are the well-known actors, actresses, athletes, entrepreneurs, musicians, and other local, national, and international figures your users will recognize and look to for guidance? You can identify these people through focus groups, interviews, and surveys, and by reviewing news and pop culture publications in your field. One drawback to using celebrities as your opinion leader is that they can easily fall out of favor. No one wants their product to be associated with a celebrity embroiled in a scandal.

- *Self-selection*—Ask for people who identify themselves as opinion leaders to come forward. Self-selection's benefits are that it's easy to implement and low cost. But this approach can be difficult due to a lack of insight into whether individuals truly are opinion leaders.

- *Self-identification*—This involves administering a questionnaire to people to determine if they qualify as opinion leaders. This is can be more reliable than self-selection, although you'll possibly have issues with reliability. Individuals might view themselves as more influential than they really are.

- *Positional*—This approach involves seeking out people holding specific positions relevant to your product's users: PTO chairperson, local politician, CEO of a major design firm, religious figures. The advantage of this method is that these people already are in the position of influence you need them to be in. The disadvantages are that these opinion leaders might not be motivated to endorse your product, and you're relying on their current position (such as clergy) to be relevant to your product.

- *User rating*—Asking users to rate the level of influence certain individuals have is another way to identify opinion leaders. This method allows you to tap directly into the thinking of your users. The drawbacks are that it can be expensive and time-consuming to use this method, and you're relying on the users you identify as being representative of the group as a whole.

## 6.3   How to design for social influence

We've reviewed key concepts related to the principle of social influence and social identity. You've probably started to make clear connections between these concepts and our more successful social platforms: Facebook, Twitter, Pinterest, and more. Let's take a closer look at how you can incorporate some of the ideas from this principle into your work.

### 6.3.1   Users want to see what they have in common with others

Designing for social identity is all about two things:

- How can you make your users feel more connected to those they're similar to?
- How can you make users feel as if your product sets them apart from those they view as different from themselves?

Your product can accomplish both of these things with multiple audiences for the same product. Facebook does this; it's their secret sauce. Facebook's design allows users to feel more connected through the ability to view and like or comment on what others in their social group are doing (figure 6.7). Users develop and strengthen their social identity and social bonds by doing this.

**Facebook allows users to engage in self-categorization; users post status updates, join groups, play games, and view content they find in line with their social identity.**

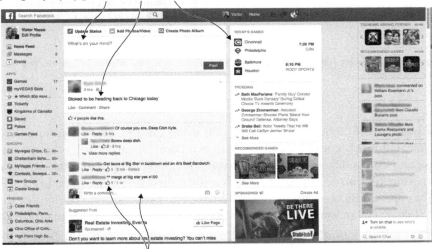

**Users reaffirm they have interests similar to others' (social comparison) when they like status updates or make positive comments on posts; likewise users can make negative comments to reinforce differences in social identity.**

**Figure 6.7   Facebook's activity feed provides users with everything they need to reaffirm their social identity.**

Facebook also allows users to create or join groups that make a strong statement about what groups they're in (figure 6.8). For example, a group with a page named People Against Baseball makes it very clear who should belong to their group (who is in-group) and who should stay away (out-group). Members of this page will engage in conversations that support their anti-baseball cause, share articles and other resources with members of the page, and attend and recommend events or meetings with members of the group. They're creating a stronger social identity and engaging in a lot of social comparison by defining who should be in their group and who should not.

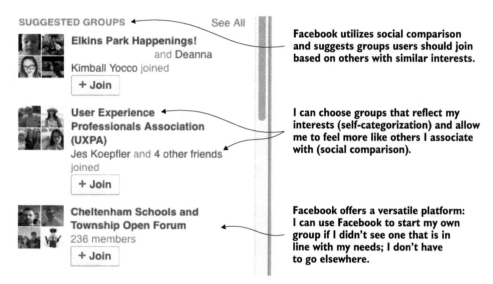

**Figure 6.8   Facebook suggests groups to join based on ones your friends belong to. You know you want to join!**

The piece that Facebook perfected is that using their platform, two opposing groups can harmoniously coexist. People Who Love Baseball can start a page, promote their cause and events, have completely separate members, recruit new members, all on the exact same platform as the group that's against their very existences. In fact, Facebook might enjoy an increase in membership based on users flocking to support their cause and show they can muster up a larger group of supporters on the platform than their opposites can. Oh, and Facebook doesn't hesitate to show you what groups your friends belong to.

**HOW TO DESIGN FOR SOCIAL IDENTITY**

Your design accounts for users' developing and deepening their social identity when you allow users to

- Create profiles others can view
- Display pictures
- Select and display personal attributes (such as a sports team fan or a movie fan)
- See activities others engage in
- View commonalities and differences with others
- Post and discuss in topical forums

### 6.3.2 Socially validating your design

Social validation is all about allowing users to see that other people use and approve of your product. Social validation can make or break your product. Positive reviews of your product can be viewed by millions of potential customers, just as easily as a negative review can go viral and stunt your product's growth. Your design, as well as your marketing plan, should account for recording and distributing product reviews or recommendations.

Mama's Vegetarian, a Philadelphia favorite, provides direct links for customers to read and post reviews on popular review websites (figure 6.9). Mama's uses this tactic to facilitate transparency about their food. Most customers have left very positive reviews. I think providing users with easy access to reviews and reviewing your product is worth the trade-off of potentially allowing a user to give you a negative review. Most users will respond positively to the gesture of providing access about your potential shortcomings as users have rated.

**Figure 6.9   Mama's Vegetarian restaurant isn't shy about linking potential customers to their reviews.**

How can you offer a space for potential users to encounter positive reviews of your product? Depending on the industry you're in, other products have done some of the heavy lifting for you. Here are three of the many options available online:

- *Angie's List*—Serves as the go-to source for reviews of service providers from verified customers
- *BBB*—Rates businesses based on frequency and number of customer complaints and their ability to resolve the complaints.
- *Glassdoor*—Focuses on employer information, including salaries, interview process, and employee reviews

### HOW TO DESIGN FOR SOCIAL VALIDATION

You should encourage users to post reviews on a designated area of your product's website for at least two reasons:

- It reflects confidence, transparency, and a willingness to stand behind your product.
- Users will find other venues to post reviews regardless. You'll save time and effort encouraging the reviews to stay close to home.

You need to

- Make it easy for users to review your product. People don't have time to post reviews about every experience they have; this means people are more likely to review an extremely positive or an extremely negative experience.
- Send users follow-up emails asking users to review your product and in the email link directly to the review page.
- Send text messages with links to reviewing your product.
- Conduct follow-up phone calls. (My car service shop does this.)
- Offer users a discount on a future purchase or entry into a contest for reviewing their experience.

When users give your product a positive review, you open up the avenue to all of their connections. This is the true beauty of social validation. If users make positive posts on your product's Facebook page, their friends might see them. If users tweet positive messages about your product, their followers might see them.

Your design should maximize the potential for positive reviews to reach all avenues of social media and public review sites.

### 6.3.3   *Getting users to comply*

Compliance has a negative connotation. People don't want to be pushed around or told what to do by overbearing salespeople. You can design for compliance in a way that enhances your users' experience.

Compliance is about how you ask your users to do something. To get our users to comply with what we're asking, we need to be straightforward about what we want them to do. If you want your users to purchase or use your product, you should be direct in how you ask. Users will respect you for that. You shouldn't attempt to force people by using veiled threats or use any type of buried text that most users overlook. For example, Hertz car rental (figure 6.10) forces users to sign up for its marketing emails if they want to have their car rental confirmation emailed. If you expect your users to appreciate gaining compliance through this type of manipulation, you're wrong. I'll unsubscribe to the next email I receive from Hertz.

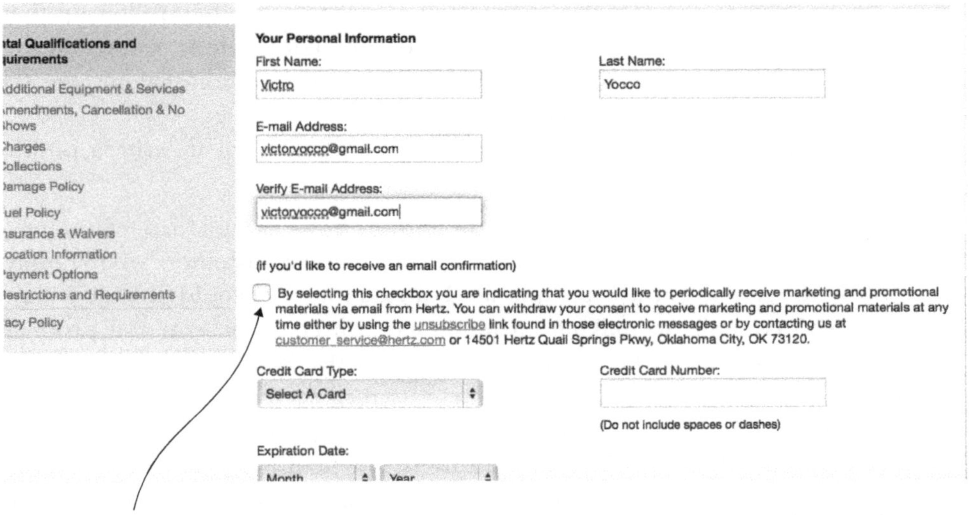

Forcing compliance is never a good idea. Hertz seems to suggest users need to opt in to receive marketing email if they want to receive a reservation confirmation email. It could also be poor alignment of the line description—which is equally as bad.

**Figure 6.10   Hertz forces me to opt in to its marketing email if I want to receive email confirmation of my rental reservation. I also misspelled my first name.**

### HOW TO DESIGN FOR COMPLIANCE

Compliance is also about *when* you ask your users to do something. You should ask users to engage in a behavior after you've created a good experience and given them an opportunity to use your product. People are more likely to comply after realizing they have an interest in, or will benefit from, use of your product.

> **NOTE**   You should present your users with a message asking them to comply with your request after you've given them a reason to want to do so.

Researchers have identified two specific compliance techniques you can incorporate in your product's experience:

- *Door-in-the-face*—This technique involves asking users to make a large commitment to your product and then reducing it to a smaller task if they say no. For example, you could ask users to purchase the full license for your product after they've given it a 10-day free trial. If the user doesn't agree, you could
  - Generate an email that offers them another 30 days of using the product at a discounted price
  - Offer them a reduced price for a limited functionality version of your product

- *Foot-in-the-door*—This is the opposite of door-in-the-face. You make a small request from users in the hopes they'll agree. You then follow up that request with more or larger requests over a period. For example, you could
  - Ask users to do something small like tweet a promotional message you've created for your product.
  - Follow up with users who comply, and ask them to write a positive review about your product.

Look for opportunities to incorporate both of these compliance techniques into the experience of your product. You should also reward customers who comply without having to use one of these techniques. For example, you could provide a discount to a user who commits to making an immediate purchase of your full product, or you could extend a user's license for a couple months free of charge. This rewards your low-maintenance customers and can activate reciprocity at a later date.

Keep in mind that it's a good policy to state upfront what you want your users to do. For example, Dogfish Head told users they had to be 21 as they asked them to comply with providing their date of birth. You should never lie to users or offer them something at a cost that you'd have given them for free.

### 6.3.4  *Encouraging users to conform*

Conformity focuses on socially acceptable behaviors. Your design should highlight how use of your product is in line with the social groups that potential users belong to. Apple does this in its iTunes application when they display the top 10 albums and singles users have downloaded (figure 6.11). Users logging in and seeing those lists are likely to explore some of this music if they think others are doing the same. Apple's top 10 lists also serve to suggest to users that many people are using iTunes to download popular music—enough that their purchases can be categorized into lists. iTunes will also recommend music based on affinity analysis—based on what others who've made similar purchases have gone on to buy.

#### HOW TO DESIGN FOR CONFORMITY

You should identify opportunities to use a method similar to Apple's to encourage conformity. Are there ways you could also display a top-sellers list that shows users that

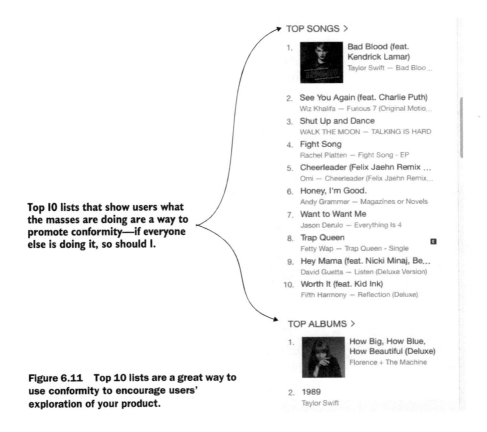

**Top 10 lists that show users what the masses are doing are a way to promote conformity—if everyone else is doing it, so should I.**

**Figure 6.11   Top 10 lists are a great way to use conformity to encourage users' exploration of your product.**

your product is among the top of your field? Perhaps you can include a list of the top features your current users access. This would encourage new users to explore these areas.

You address conformity in your design when you include elements like

- Top 10 lists
- Affinity recommendations (based on relationships between users)
- Feeds/updates showing what others are doing
- Peer review and recommendations

If you have members of diverse interest groups that use your product, you can

- Create pages where members of these groups can engage in a discussion about your product, similar to Facebook's page
- Reference this area when you market your product and on various pages throughout the experience ("See what other members of our Fans of XYZ are talking about")

### 6.3.5  *Harnessing the power of opinion leaders*

You stand to gain a large following for your product if you can tap into opinion leaders. The first step you should take is to identify opinion leaders who are relevant to the use of your product. Take a structured approach to identifying opinion leaders. It's not helpful to use an opinion leader who isn't in line with your audience. LeBron James (figure 6.12) is hardly going to be the main influence as to what type of software the cross-stitch of the month club uses to create its patterns. Sure, LeBron is an opinion leader, but not when it comes to cross-stitching.

Figure 6.12  LeBron James can influence your users' opinions on basketball shoes, but can he slam-dunk his way into the hearts of cross-stitchers?

#### HOW TO DESIGN USING OPINION LEADERS

Your design might feature opinion leaders in a number of ways, but you also want to highlight the fact that opinion leaders are using your product. You can

- Identify the correct opinion leaders to access using the advice in section 6.2.5.
- Display opinion leaders' testimonials about using your product on your site.
- Promote opinion leaders' public use of your product through videos you post online.
- Use opinion leaders as a distribution point for your product; have them attend events or make public appearances with links and discount codes for using your product.

## 6.4   *Talking the talk: Conversations about social influence*

There are many ways to discuss social influence with your clients. Most of your clients will be aware of the importance of positive reviews, social media, and Facebook-type interactions of commenting and sharing. Here are some examples of ways you can discuss designing for social influence:

- *Social influence*—"We know that your users would like to form groups with similar interests. We've created an area where users can join groups around their interests. We're encouraging friendly competition by allowing the groups to issue challenges to each other. Whichever group wins the challenge will have a badge icon added to their group page for others to see when browsing."
- *Opinion leader*—"We've polled your users to find out who they consider influential leaders in their local community. We recommend contacting these leaders and asking them to use your product. We can train them to make them proficient at use, and then ask them to recommend the product to others and help them learn to use it."
- *Social validation*—"Your users are very vocal about your product. We've designed an area to capture user feedback. We've also designed emails that will ask users that if they're satisfied to please leave a review. Users can also tweet their rating and the tweets can be compiled on a separate page within the review area."

## 6.5   *Case study: Drought shaming*

The state of California experienced a prolonged period of severe drought through the summer of 2015. The drought devastated many of California's crops, and lakes and streams were drying up. The state issued mandatory water restrictions, attempting to force local communities to monitor and reduce residents' water usage.

Many Californians were used to watering their lawns, washing their cars, and participating in other high-intensity water usage activities whenever they wanted. State and local governments had difficulty changing these behaviors. Authorities had little power to limit individual water usage, with the exception of issuing fines.

Water or drought shaming (#droughtshaming) became a Twitter phenomenon where individuals in drought-stricken areas of California would post photos or videos of people and businesses overusing water or violating water restrictions. Drought shaming capitalized on many of the concepts of the principle of social influence you've learned in this chapter.

Users contributing to drought shaming over social media hoped to influence members of their social groups to pressure the individuals or businesses being shamed, while also hoping the social nature of the shaming would influence the individual or business to reduce water usage in the future.

The creators of VizSafe, an app designed to allow community members to share and report what's taking place in their community, realized the importance of social influence and the drought-shaming phenomenon. VizSafe quickly designed an updated section of its product to allow users to post pictures and comments related to community members wasting water (figure 6.13).

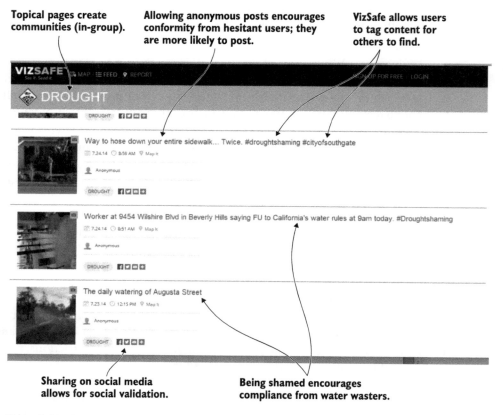

**Figure 6.13    VizSafe effectively captures many components of social identity and social influence to increase use of its product around topics like #droughtshaming.**

Let's review how drought shaming on VizSafe and Twitter addressed a number of the concepts we've covered this chapter.

### 6.5.1    Social Identity Theory and drought shaming

Individuals participating in drought shaming have gone through both categorization and comparison.

#### SELF-CATEGORIZATION

Individuals posting pictures and messages shaming on VizSafe or Twitter categorized themselves as members of a group taking on the responsibility of monitoring others' behaviors, as being concerned about the impact of the drought on their local community, and as believing in the power of social media to affect change.

Individuals being shamed were members of a group of people who, knowingly or not, were potentially violating local and state water restrictions. I can't say whether these people were aware they were in violation of the restrictions. They might've been unaware members of a group that others attached negative feelings toward. If local water authorities had warned a member of this group and that individual continued with the behavior, then the person was willingly categorizing him- or herself as an overuser in purposeful violation of water restrictions.

Both of these groups could've started a Facebook page!

### SOCIAL COMPARISON

Members of the group who participated in drought shaming categorized themselves as being part of a group living in a drought-stricken area and complying with the local and state water regulations. They were also users of smartphone applications or social media, such as Twitter (figure 6.14), which is where much of the shaming occurred. People sharing these characteristics were considered in-group, as would others who were complying with water regulations.

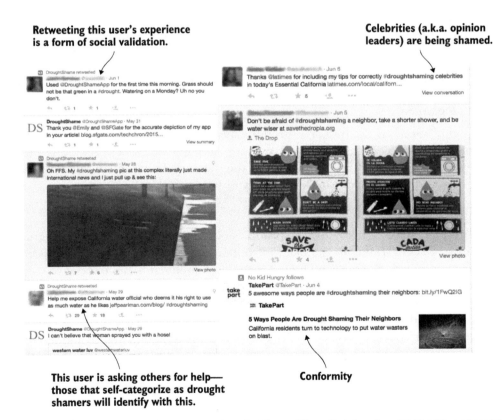

**Retweeting this user's experience is a form of social validation.**

**Celebrities (a.k.a. opinion leaders) are being shamed.**

**This user is asking others for help—those that self-categorize as drought shamers will identify with this.**

**Conformity**

**Figure 6.14   Drought-shaming tweets take advantage of the principles of social identity and social influence.**

You didn't have to shame others to be a member of the drought shamers. You could be a passive participant if you viewed or privately shared the shaming messages. You were also in-group if you complied with water regulations. Drought shamers identified one specific out-group: those not complying with water usage restrictions. The characteristics of this out-group included having lush green lawns in drought-stricken areas; overusing water for washing cars, clothes, or other household tasks; taking long showers; and not installing low-flow faucets or shower heads throughout their house. Individuals engaging in these behaviors were categorized as out-group.

### 6.5.2 *Social validation*

Drought shaming relied on social validation as the key concept involved in increasing levels of drought shaming, preventing water overuse, and changing behaviors. Individuals making shaming posts and claims found that others validated their opinions and supported drought shaming. This encouraged additional posts and monitoring of others, as the validation from social networks provided an incentive. National media contributed to social validation: CNBC, local NBC news channels, *USA Today*, the *Washington Post*, and many more all ran stories on drought shaming.

Individuals who experienced shaming were socially invalidated in the way a one-star rating of an application would damage the reputation of the app. Individuals worried about their social status, who could see their pictures online, would want to stop their water overuse. According to some drought shamers, the purpose of shaming was for the offenders to seek education or become more aware of their behavior.

### 6.5.3 *Compliance*

Compliance was the outcome drought shamers sought. They wanted the offending parties to stop engaging in water overuse. Drought shamers were asking for compliance in a public way, in the hopes that the shame of being called out in front of their peers would force individuals to comply with the water policies.

### 6.5.4 *Conformity*

Drought shaming provides two examples of conformity. First, those doing the shaming were conforming to the behavior others had originally started. The more people shamed others, the more people engaged in shaming; it became socially acceptable to shame people for water overuse. If no one had paid attention to the shaming and no one else had engaged in shaming, the behavior of shaming wouldn't have spread. Social media gave potential users a reference point for how much shaming was happening and who was doing the shaming. Potential shamers could search for #droughtshaming on Twitter and other social media, as well as look at the ratings and popularity of apps such as VizSafe that were being used to engage in shaming.

### 6.5.5 *Opinion leaders*

Opinion leaders played an interesting role in drought shaming. Drought shamers turned the tables on celebrities who were overusing water. Many of these celebrities would typically have been considered opinion leaders. Instead, drought shamers called attention to the privilege many celebrities believed they enjoyed. Drought shamers used the celebrities' status as a means of drawing additional attention to their cause. Shaming a celebrity was likely to have a greater impact than shaming your average next-door neighbor.

## 6.6 *End-of-chapter exercise*

You're heading up a design team tasked with creating an app that focuses on getting users to live healthier lifestyles. You can focus on a number of health-related issues, from increasing exercise, promoting a healthy diet, or gaining better control over health issues (such as diabetes). The choice is yours. Sketch out the general idea of your application and its design, and then answer the questions that follow. You can share your answers and provide feedback on the Manning Publications forum here: https://forums.manning.com/forums/design-for-the-mind.

- How might some of your users categorize themselves?
- How can you increase the diversity of your users and potential users?
- How does use of your product set your users apart from other groups?
- How might you facilitate multiple groups (perhaps even opposites such as Facebook) using your product?
- What form of social validation would be most beneficial and how would you provide opportunities for social validation (such as sharing, liking, or reviewing)?
- Who are opinion leaders in your field? How can you provide them with insight into using your product?
- How might your design use compliance and conformity to promote use?

## 6.7 *Additional resources*

Cialdini, R.B., and N.J. Goldstein. (2004). Social influence: Compliance and conformity. *Annual Review of Psychology*, 55, 591–621. (A paper identifying the motivations individuals have for complying and conforming to the opinions of others.)

Tajfel, H., and J.C. Turner. (1979). An integrative theory of intergroup conflict. *The Social Psychology of Intergroup Relations*, 33(47), 74. (Tajfel and Turner's classic paper on Social Identity Theory.)

Valente, T.W., and P. Pumpuang. (2007). Identifying opinion leaders to promote behavior change. *Health Education & Behavior*, 34, 881–896. (An excellent paper for describing how to identify group opinion leaders.)

Wood, W. (2000). Attitude change: Persuasion and social influence. *Annual Review of Psychology*, 51(1), 539–570. (A review of literature on social influence and persuasion.)

KEYWORDS: compliance and conformity, opinion leaders, Social Identity Theory, social influence, social networks

## 6.8    Summary

- Users create a social identity through self-categorization and social comparison.
- Self-categorization is when individuals categorize themselves as similar based on certain characteristics they align with; your design should include opportunities for users to identify with a number of traits.
- Social comparison is when individuals look at others and say they are either like (in-group) or unlike (out-group) these others; your design should make it clear how users would align themselves with others.
- Social validation, compliance, and conformity are other key components of influence.
- Social validation is the act of individuals looking at what others they view as members of their social group recommend or dislike; your design can allow for social validation through liking, reviewing, and sharing.
- Compliance involves individuals agreeing to do something because they're asked to do it; you design for compliance when you ask a user to engage in a task.
- Conformity involves an individual following what others are doing; your design accounts for conformity when you show users what others are doing.

# It's not what you say;
# it's how you say it!

**This chapter covers**

- Framing communication to users and potential users
- Ensuring your design accommodates effective framing of communication
- Identifying areas of improvement to frame communication to users
- Discussing framing with others
- Effectively framing communication in digital contexts

Gen. Smythe is a 20-year Army veteran. He receives an email from a local candidate asking him to download a tablet application that will track all of the candidates his party has running in the local, state, and national election. The email contains a picture of the candidate and the message "Download our XYZ Party app to make sure you stay up to date with the latest candidates and issues." Gen. Smythe deletes the email and doesn't think about downloading the app.

Two weeks later, Gen. Smythe gets an email from the headquarters of the local candidate of the party in which he's a registered voter. This email contains a graphic of the American flag, a bald eagle, an apple pie, fireworks, and Uncle Sam.

The caption under the graphic asks Gen. Smythe to "Do your patriotic duty: download this app and vote for the candidates and issues that keep our country great." Gen. Smythe immediately downloads the app and registers his personal information so that he can get accurate information on local candidates and issues.

Both scenarios involved the same app. The first scenario failed to effectively frame the information. The second application framed the information in a way that was understandable and motivational to Gen. Smythe. The framing effects of the email caused the general to develop a positive attitude toward the app and subsequently the behavior of downloading and using the app.

How we communicate our design matters almost as much as what we're communicating. We frame discussions around our design through the interactions and work-flows we create, the visuals we attach to our design, and the words we use to communicate to our users. Framing communication involves setting the tone in which you want users to receive and interpret your message. Effective framing (figure 7.1) can lead to users engaging with, or increasing use of, your design.

**NOTE**    Framing communication is relevant to every principle we've covered in this book. We frame all information we communicate to our users and our peers. We set the tone for every other psychological principle when we frame the information we present to users. We can show users we intend to create a social experience (chapter 6), an experience that will increase their control (chapter 2), an experience that will utilize the scarcity heuristic (chapter 3), and every other principle in this book by using the correct frame of communication.

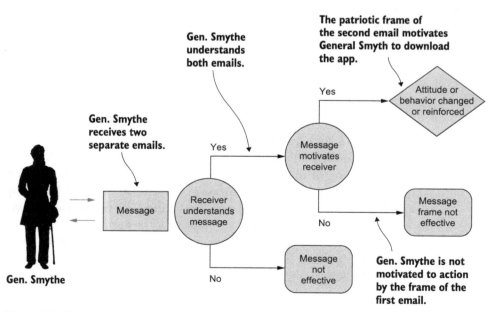

**Figure 7.1   How users encounter and process framed messages**

## 7.1    Introduction

We can discuss a topic, product, or concept in many ways. Framing isn't about adding additional information to your core message, but how you explain, or *frame*, your core message. Researchers have spent countless hours and dollars examining the frames of communication that exist, how they're used, and which frames are effective at motivating people.

### 7.1.1    Brief academic background

Researchers have spent decades examining the effects of framing communication. Much of what we know about framing comes from studies of media and politics. Both of these fields tend to frame an issue in multiple ways. For example, one study found that many people who were surveyed would gladly support "a program offering short-term assistance to families who have fallen on hard times" but that they'd be strongly against "a program offering handouts to those who aren't working." Both statements are talking about the same issue—public welfare policy—but the frame of communication used brings up completely different images of the purpose of the program.

Dennis Chong and James Druckman from Northwestern University have focused their careers on identifying the effects of frames of communication on public opinion. The researchers were interested in finding out what happens when someone encounters two strongly framed messages with opposing views about the same topic. This would simulate a real-life situation such as an election season where the public encounters multiple contradictory messages from politicians about the same topic.

Druckman conducted a study using messages framed for and against a measure allowing casino gambling. He found that participants receiving only one message strongly framed for or against the casino saw a significant shift in their attitude toward the direction of the message (for or against a casino). But when people received two strongly framed messages that opposed each other, there was no significant shift in attitudes. The messages canceled each other out. Also, if someone received a strong message framed for or against casinos and then a weak message with the opposite frame, participants attitudes shifted in the direction of the strong message. This highlights the importance of creating well-framed messages. You can nullify or override messages framed by competing products if you frame your communication effectively.

The Centers for Disease Control (CDC) takes the findings from research on framing communication seriously. The CDC uses research-based frames to shape its communication on public health issues such as avoiding smoking (section 7.5). It attempts to guide local health organizations on creating strongly framed messages in order to overcome attitudes against certain public health issues like getting children vaccinated to prevent outbreaks of measles.

## 7.2    Key concepts of framing communication

Effectively framed messages need to account for two key factors in the individual receiving the message: understanding and motivation.

### 7.2.1 People need to understand the message

The person receiving the message needs to understand what the message is about, both the topic and the frame being used. For example, the Mr. Yuk face (figure 7.2) that was commonly used to designate poisonous substances from my youth might not convey the warning frame to someone who's never heard of or encountered Mr. Yuk. For those familiar with Mr. Yuk and the underlying concept that he represents toxic material, the frame helps even those without the ability to read to understand there's danger in the material they're handling.

Figure 7.2    Mr. Yuk is used to frame communication warning youngsters not to ingest chemicals.

### 7.2.2 People need to be motivated by the message

Motivation means that the message needs to be framed in a way that motivates the receiver to do, or not to do, a certain action. Looking at Mr. Yuk again, the initial frame communicates danger to a person handling or thinking about consuming a toxic substance. This is a warning *not* to ingest poison. If someone has ingested the substance, the message is framed to make someone else aware that this person has consumed poison and motivate him or her to seek treatment for the person.

Please note that I'll refer to framing your "message" and "communication" for the remainder of this chapter, but I'm not referring simply to words. We communicate messages through everything we put in front of our users—colors, interactions, and workflows; visual aids/cues and iconography; our navigation; and the terminology we use. There is, after all, a good reason for Mr. Yuk to be green and have a distinct facial expression.

## 7.3 How to design for framing communication

You have many options when it comes to framing communication to your users. Framing communication should be a part of your overall content strategy. There's no single correct way to frame communication—but you can't effectively communicate your values to others without accounting for their values. You should conduct research with users to understand how to best communicate your message to them, as well as test your messages to ensure they're effectively conveying what you want your users to understand. I'll discuss research more in sections 7.3.2 and 7.3.6.

Here's a strategy I suggest for developing a well-framed message:

1 Identify what you want to communicate.
2 Conduct research to determine users' feelings toward and knowledge of your product.

3  Choose a framing technique.
4  Choose your frame of communication.
5  Create your message.
6  Test your message.
7  Release your well-framed message.

You can add as many steps to this strategy as you'd like, but covering these seven steps will ensure that you account for the basics of a well-framed message. Let's cover these steps in more detail.

### 7.3.1  Identify what you want to communicate

This first step is often overlooked, or underemphasized, when we set out to design our message. We often assume that everyone on our team is on the same page in terms of what it is we want to communicate to our users. I recommend beginning any design project with a discussion among key team members to determine what the key message is that you're trying to communicate to your users. You'll avoid mixed messages or lack of cohesion in your messaging when you work as a team to identify this first. Here are some potential messages you might be trying to communicate:

- A specific action you want users to engage in
- Your product's ease of use
- Your product's new features
- Your product's security features
- Your company's values

### 7.3.2  User research

Be sure to use a trained researcher to conduct research with users. Your team should work with the researcher (who ideally is already part of the team) to define what you'd like to understand about users before creating your message. Your research needs to answer the following questions:

- What are common misconceptions about your product?
- How do your users receive communication about your product?
- What framing techniques (see section 7.3.3) might be most effective with your users?
- What frames of communication (see section 7.3.4) might be most effective with your users?
- What opportunities exist to educate potential users about your product?
- How can you create a message your users will understand?
- What are the best ways to motivate potential and current users to use your product more?

Your researcher will work to shape the questions and potential prompts that will get you the most valuable information from users. Once you and your researcher analyze your data, you can make better informed decisions for the next steps.

### 7.3.3  *Choose a framing technique*

Before you think about which frame of communication to use (section 7.3.4), you'll need to decide which technique you'll use to frame your message. Scholars Fairhurst and Sarr (1996; see the additional resources) identify seven framing techniques.

#### ARTIFACT

Artifacts are objects that have symbolic value; visual/symbolic value is greater than the object itself. Many of the objects in design are artifacts. Smartphone icons are artifacts. There's no inherent value to an icon, but we assign a symbolic value, including functions (for example, a camera representing the camera iOS app, and the camera representing the Instagram app, as shown in figure 7.3).

Figure 7.3  Icons are examples of artifacts: we've attached symbolic value to them, and they're more than just pictures.

#### CONTRAST

Contrast describes something in terms of what it isn't. Infographics can often visually contrast information between two or more things. For years, Verizon Wireless has used a map of its coverage in contrast to the coverage of other U.S. cell phone carriers as a framing technique (figure 7.4).

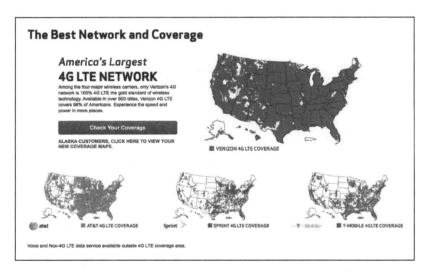

Figure 7.4  Verizon Wireless contrasts its coverage area with that of its competition.

#### METAPHOR

A metaphor involves comparing a concept to something else. We frequently use metaphors in marketing: for example, Prudential Insurance claims to be a rock (strong, sturdy, and safe), whereas Skittles claims you can taste the rainbow when you eat its variety of fruity flavors (figure 7.5).

Prudential =
a rock

Skittles =
a rainbow

**Figure 7.5   Marketing design often uses metaphors. Prudential displays a rock to convey the strength and reliability of its company, whereas Skittles uses a rainbow as a metaphor for the variety of fruity flavors its product has.**

### SLOGAN OR CATCHPHRASE

You can use a catchy phrase to make something more memorable or relatable. Using our example from figure 7.5, Prudential has the slogan "Bring your challenges" built right into its brand logo, and Skittles invites consumers to "Taste the rainbow."

Do you have a catchy phrase you can add to messages about your product to make them more memorable? If you do, you need to use it consistently across mediums, or consumers and potential consumers will become confused. Also, avoid changing it too often if you want to build and maintain brand recognition.

### STORIES

Stories use narrative in a vivid and memorable way. Designers use infographics to tell stories. For example, History.com uses an infographic to tell the story of humankind by the numbers (figure 7.6), in which they look at population growth and other interesting facts related to the population of humans around the world.

### SPIN

Spin presents a concept in a way that conveys a value. Spin doesn't necessarily mean lying to people, but it's a form of propaganda. Putting spin on an issue means you're creating a situation in which users

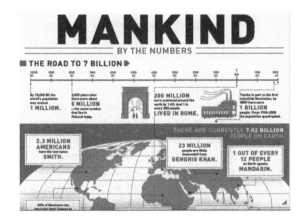

**Figure 7.6   Infographics help tell stories using visual aids. History.com uses an infographic to discuss interesting population characteristics as our world grows toward overpopulation. See http://mng.bz/pMoL.**

will view your design or product as something positive and something else as negative. For example, www.juststand.org provides an infographic on the unhealthy nature of sitting. Juststand.org (figure 7.7) would have people attach an extremely negative value on sitting, and a positive value to its solution—standing, particularly at a standing desk. If you dig a little deeper, you'll see that www.juststand.org/ isn't an impartial organization. It is a property of Ergotron, a maker of standing desks.

**Figure 7.7   Juststand.org spins sitting as the unhealthiest activity you can engage in. Unfortunately, they lose credibility when you realize they're a property of a private company that produces standing desks.**

### TRADITION

Traditions are long-established customs and beliefs. Traditions can be difficult, because many are unique to specific cultures and regions, or even subgroups within cultures. You'll need to conduct thorough research if you plan to insert tradition into your communication—partly to make sure folks will understand what you're presenting them with, and partly to make sure you won't offend users who don't share similar traditions. For example, many people hold the tradition that marriage is solely between a man and a woman. The man wears a black tux-

**Figure 7.8   You might need to update your clip art symbolizing the tradition of marriage.**

edo, the woman wears a white dress (figure 7.8), and they get married in a church. We've seen a shift in this tradition in the United States, with same-sex marriages now recognized, not to mention the fact that people are very eclectic in their wedding dress and locations. If your technique involves accessing a tradition such as marriage, you'll need to shift your visuals as the tradition shifts.

### 7.3.4   *Choose your frame of communication*

You'll need to choose a frame of communication that will help motivate your users to engage in the behavior you want them to. There are many frames of communication; I'm going to cover three very large categories that are particularly relevant to design. You can use the additional resources to explore frames beyond the three I cover here. You should utilize the data from research with users to help determine the frame of communication you choose. I also suggest designing messages using multiple frames—the more the merrier—to promote the behavior you want users to engage in.

**GAIN-BASED FRAME**

A gain-based frame is exactly what it sounds like; your message focuses on what positive outcome users stand to gain from your product. You should identify what these gains are ahead of time, so that you aren't promising something that won't happen. Gains can include access to resources, knowledge, memories, money, peers, productivity, positive emotions/experiences time, and anything else your product might allow users to increase. Apptrailer.com (figure 7.9) uses artifacts to tell a gain-framed story to communicate the value of its reward points to potential users of its app.

**Figure 7.9   Apptrailer.com uses artifacts and a story to convey a gain-based framed message.**

**LOSS-BASED FRAME**

Loss-based frames focus on what won't happen or what will be lost if the message receiver doesn't engage in an action. You can use loss-based frames to activate individuals' loss aversion, as I discussed in chapter 3. Medical personnel often focus on loss-based frames—for example, telling people they're likely to become sick or die early (loss of health and life) if they overconsume alcohol on a regular basis.

Overstock.com (figure 7.10) uses a loss-based frame in communicating to users that the company wants to sign up for its rewards account. Overstock.com tracks users' orders and displays the amount of money users would've saved if they were enrolled in the rewards program. They're literally showing users exactly what they're losing.

**Overstock.com uses a loss-base framed message to motivate me to join their rewards club; the fact that they can tell me exactly how many rewards I've missed out on makes this message potentially more effective than a generic message.**

Figure 7.10   Overstock.com uses a loss-based frame message to motivate users signing up for its rewards program.

### VALUE-BASED FRAMES

You could choose to focus on appealing to users' values through your message's frame. Researchers have identified many value-based frames, including

- *Conservative*—Conservative values in the United States include preservation of traditional norms, a free-market approach to the economy, smaller government, the right to bear arms, and a strong national defense. Many conservative framed messages involve spinning the message to promote conservative ideals. The National Association for Gun Rights is a conservative organization. Most of the messages on its website (figure 7.11) are framed with conservative values, which appeal to users and potential members.

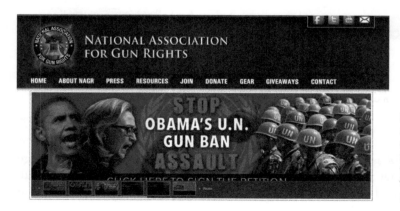

Figure 7.11   The National Association for Gun Rights, a conservative organization, frames its message using conservative values to tell a story asking users to sign a petition against liberal politicians.

- *Liberal*—Liberal values in the United States include that government should ensure citizens' rights are protected against corporations, that governments should guarantee public welfare and a decent standard of living, and that governments and public policy should intervene as necessary to ensure society functions well. Many liberal framed messages involve spinning the message to promote liberal ideals. The American Civil Liberties Union (ACLU) is a liberal organization that uses the powers of the judicial system (lawsuits) to call attention to areas in which they feel governments aren't effectively protecting citizens' rights. Most of the messages on the ACLU website (figure 7.12) are framed with liberal values.

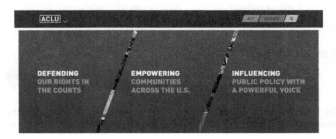

Figure 7.12  The ACLU uses a liberal frame to tell the story of the purpose of its organization: court intervention, community organization, and public policy to protect citizens are typically liberal values in the United States.

- *Altruistic*—Altruism is a trait in which a person places more value on the well being of others. Altruistic value frames appeal to users who are empathetic to others, or who are more concerned for the welfare of their family. Altruistic frames don't appeal to people who are self-centered. Organdonor.gov (figure 7.13) appeals to users with a number of altruistic framed stories designed to motivate users to register as organ donors.

Figure 7.13  Organdonor.gov uses stories framed with altruistic values to appeal to potential donors. Note that it uses a parental frame as well for one story; use of multiple frames isn't an uncommon practice.

- *Parental*—Parental frames focus on activating parental feelings in users. Messages using a parental frame often feature children or animals (or a lethal combination of children and animals—no one can say no to a message with a kid holding a puppy). You should note that the parental frame might be ineffective when used on someone who doesn't have experience with or interest in children. State Farm uses a simple picture of a man meant to be the father or guardian of children (figure 7.14). Users open to the parental frame instantly understand the connection between life insurance and protecting your children should you die.

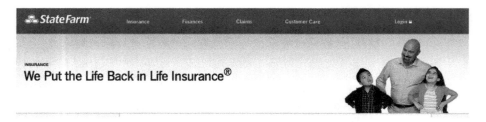

**Figure 7.14    State Farm displays children with an adult (I'm assuming a parent) to use a parental frame to tell the story that life insurance is important for the sake of your children.**

- *Religious*—Religious-based frames focus on evoking religious figures, imagery, or passages from religious texts as a way of framing a message. There are many religions, and religion is a contentious subject. If you choose to use a religious frame, you'll likely turn away a number of users regardless of how open-minded your message is. That said, there should be many ways to frame a religious message that's receptive to members of other religions/nonreligious users. Oklahoma Wesleyan (figure 7.15) uses artifacts (symbols) as well as tradition (the tradition of a religion) to tell the Christianity framed story of its campus.

**Figure 7.15    Oklahoma Wesleyan immediately presents users with a religious (Christianity) framed story.**

**HUMAN FRAME**

Human frames are unique to digital contexts and ones where users are communicating through an electronic interface. A human frame presents data to users in a way that projects a more human approach—data with feelings, so to speak. We see this when websites provide a picture of a customer service rep next to the text entry box, or even better, when they allow for a video connection between you and the rep.

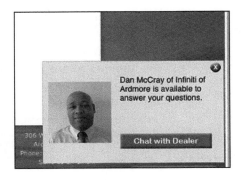

**Figure 7.16   Infiniti makes me feel like I'm speaking with a person I've met by providing me with a picture of the person I'm supposedly interacting with online.**

Infiniti provides a picture of the dealer you're supposedly communicating with (figure 7.16). A human frame helps to establish the relationship you expect when considering a large purchase such as car or home.

Compare the warm feeling of the human frame in the previous figure with the cold, standoffish feeling of the robotic framed message in figure 7.17. Everything from the font, to the block word-wall layout, to the unfriendly language causes readers to feel they're interacting with a machine and not a person. I had no desire to open the attachments to this email—attachments that contained important messages—given the formatting felt like spam.

```
This message was originally submitted by local activities@HQ.ACM.ORG to the
SIGCHI-PHILADELPHIA-OFFICERS list at LISTSERV.ACM.ORG. You can approve it using
the "OK" mechanism (click on the link below), ignore it, or repost an edited
copy. The message will expire automatically. You do not need to do anything if
you just want to discard it. Please refer to the List Owner's Manual at
http://www.lsoft.com/resources/manuals.asp if you are not familiar with the
"OK" mechanism. These instructions are being kept purposefully short for your
convenience in processing large numbers of messages.

To APPROVE the message:
http://listserv.acm.org/SCRIPTS/WA-ACMLPX.CGI?OK=0A128258&L=SIGCHI-PHILADELPHIA-OFFICERS
```

**Figure 7.17   This autogenerated message contained an attachment with the actual message from a real person; however, the instructions given in this message do not refer to the fact that a message from a human is attached. This message is from the Association for Computing Machinery Computer Human Interaction special interest group—you'd think they would know how to better frame a message from a computer.**

### 7.3.5   Create your message

You should craft a number of potential versions of your message using the framing technique(s) and frame(s) your research has found likely to be effective. Your team can work together to create the messages, or you can have one person create the messages and others review them. Either way, I recommend working with a content strategist who will have the skills to make sure messages are consistent, are pushed to the right channels, and are helping with your overall product strategy.

I recommend creating more than one message, using multiple techniques and frames. You can use several messages to say the same thing, particularly if using multiple mediums to share your message. You might tell a gain-framed story on your homepage, expand on this story with a blog post, shorten it to a catchphrase in a banner ad and tweet it, and then post an artifact on dribble.

Creating multiple messages allows you to have options as you enter the next step: testing your message.

### 7.3.6    *Test your message*

Be sure to test your message with a sample of users or potential users. Don't be overly concerned about the sample size, but do pay attention to the types of users you sample. You'll find any issues related to lack of clarity in your message with a sample as small as five.

#### COMPARISON TESTING

Comparison testing involves researchers having users or potential users compare multiple messages on the same topic. This is the ideal method for confirming the most effective frame if you're trying to narrow down your messages. Recruit participants who meet the profile of the users you're creating the message for. If your product is business software meant to track staff members' time spent on specific projects, you'd want to recruit people who work in an environment where they take part in several projects and track their time. Your researcher can help with accessing the appropriate population.

Next, you should test at least two versions of the same message with different users. For example, here are two versions of a message; the first uses a gain-based frame (use gains time) and the second is framed with a loss-based frame (lack of use loses time):

- Using the TimeTracker2000 will save you time tracking how long you work on projects and allow you to record your time spent on projects without error.
- Not using TimeTracker2000 could cost you extra time tracking how long you work on projects and require you to redo data entry should errors occur.

Your researcher can develop questions to identify which message resonates stronger.

#### MESSAGE EVALUATION

You can use as few as five participants to effectively evaluate a message. For this method, you can present the same participant with as many messages as you choose; you won't be comparing the effectiveness of the messages against each other. Your researcher will work with your team to develop questions to identify the following:

- What parts of each message do users find confusing (understanding)?
- What do users think each message is asking them to do (motivation)?
- What parts of each message do users feel are effective?

Your researcher should analyze the data and report on the findings as recommendations for modifications to strengthen each message.

### 7.3.7   *Release your well-framed message*

Now it's time to release your message(s) to the world. You should strategically determine when to release the message. You wouldn't want to ask people to download an app before it's available. You should also come to a consensus on how (which mediums or channels) you'll communicate your message. Again, I strongly recommend having a content strategist on your team to track the communication strategy and make sure it's consistent across messages and mediums.

## 7.4   *Talking the talk: Conversations about framing communication*

You'll need to communicate the purpose of the framing techniques and frames you're using. This will help to ensure consistency in messaging across team members. Fortunately, you can easily convey the basics of framing communication to most people familiar with creating or receiving messages on design-focused topics. Here are some examples of how you can communicate your choice of frames to your peers or clients. I've provided some examples based on a scenario where you're designing a banking application with integrated personal financial management functionality:

- *Gain-based artifact*—"Our research with users found that they view the use of your product as a way to gain control over their finances and spending habits. We're going to communicate these gains in our messages to users. We also found that users are very familiar with the dollar sign icon representing a positive relationship with money. So when we have users move their money into savings, the icon to access that area is a large dollar sign with the caption 'Increase my savings!'"
- *Loss-based story*—"We're surfacing information on how much money users spend on nonessential items in a way that will make it clear they might consider reducing their spending to increase savings. For example, if users purchase coffee three times a day on average, they'll get a message at the end of the month that states purchasing coffee has cost you $x.xx. This cost is reducing the amount of money you're able to put toward your savings goal. Are there ways you might reduce your spending on coffee?"

You should also use framing to your advantage when you discuss design feature recommendations with your clients or peers. For example, instead of saying, "I think users will really appreciate the ability to have single sign-on access to their accounts," you can say, "We'll increase users' satisfaction with your products if we can offer single sign-on." Alternatively, you can try, "User satisfaction will suffer if we don't offer single sign-on."

Pay attention to how you frame your communication throughout your daily interactions. You'll soon see that the person you're talking to and the subject you're talking about often dictate the frame you use. Ask yourself whether the frame(s) you currently use are getting the results you want. When you're consciously aware of the fames you use, you have the ability to choose a more effective frame for motivating the behavior you want from others.

## 7.5    *Case study: BeTobaccoFree.gov*

The U.S. Department of Health and Human Services' CDC has invested millions of dollars conducting research on how to frame messages. This makes a lot of sense, because the CDC needs to effectively communicate with a large number of people (the world!) about the need to take action related to health issues: everything from epidemics like Ebola, to more common health-related behaviors like getting a mammogram.

Smoking cigarettes is a behavior that has been on the CDC's naughty list for quite a while. The CDC uses a mix of gain- and loss-based artifacts, stories, spin, and tradition to present gain-, loss-, and value-based framed messages to users. The website is extremely comprehensive, and I recommend spending time examining the CDC's anti-smoking material on BeTobaccoFree.gov for an in-depth review of message framing.

### 7.5.1    *A variety of frames: The buckshot approach*

BeTobaccoFree.gov uses a buckshot approach to framing messages on several pages of its website (figure 7.18). This means they're using multiple framing techniques and frames at one time in an attempt to appeal to the greatest number of users. This approach might be effective for issues like smoking, but it might not be the best approach for your design. I strongly recommend following through with message testing to make sure your frames speak to your users.

**Figure 7.18   The CDC's "buckshot" approach uses multiple techniques and multiple frames to promote negative attitudes toward smoking.**

### GAIN- AND LOSS-BASED FRAMES

BeTobaccoFree.gov uses gain- and loss-based frames for most of its messages focusing on quitting or not starting smoking. The loss-based messages focus on the negative impacts on health of smoking, as well as the financial cost of smoking cigarettes. The gain-based framed messages focus on the positive impact quitting smoking has on your health, and the amount of money saved when you quit smoking.

### PARENTAL FRAME

BeTobaccoFree.gov uses the parental frame throughout its site (figure 7.19). We're well aware of the negative effects of smoking on unborn children; these messages serve to persuade women who are pregnant or looking to become pregnant to quit smoking, or not to start.

## Smoking Affects Your Pregnancy

**Figure 7.19   The CDC uses parental framed messages to warn pregnant women and potentially pregnant women of the dangers of smoking.**

### 7.5.2    *Is the CDC's approach effective?*

The CDC's effort, as part of a broader effort, seems to be effective. U.S. smoking rates have dropped from 21 percent in 2005 to under 18 percent in 2013. This amounts to millions and millions of fewer Americans smoking. Even better, the CDC reports that 2013 data shows the rate of teenage smokers in the United States hit a record low of 15.7 percent.

## 7.6    *End-of-chapter exercise: Find a frame that works!*

As an exercise, sketch a message addressing the prompt. You can share your answers and provide feedback on the Manning Publications forum here: https://forums.manning.com/forums/design-for-the-mind.

1   Create a loss-based frame to communicate why a 10-year-old should do his or her homework.

2   Create a gain-based frame for an adult to participate in an after-work softball club.

3   Choose any value-based frame to create a message convincing people they should use a new word processing application.

4   How would you reframe the message from figure 7.17 to make it friendlier to users?

Answer the following questions as they relate to a project you've recently worked on:

1   What artifacts are relevant to the topic your design addresses?

2   How might you tell a story using a gain-based frame?

3   What traditions relate to use of your product?

4   What value-based frames might be most effective for motivating your users?

## 7.7    *Additional resources*

Cho, H., and F.J. Boster. (2008). Effects of gain versus loss frame antidrug ads on adolescents. *Journal of Communication*, 58(3), 428–446. (An article that examines the effects of gain versus loss frames on adolescents. Adolescents that reported they have friends who use drugs were more persuaded by loss-based framed messages.)

Chong, D., and J.N. Druckman. (2007). Framing theory. *Annual Review of Political Science* 10, 103–126. (Chong and Druckman explore how and why framing works to persuade people.)

Fairhurst, G. and R. Sarr. 1996. *The art of framing.* San Francisco: Jossey-Bass. (An exploration of framing from a leadership perspective. This book uses real-life examples to show how well-thought-out, powerful frames of communication can motivate people and inspire action.)

Grantham, S., L. Ahern and C. Connolly-Ahern. (2011). Merck's one less campaign: Using risk message frames to promote the use of Gardasil® in HPV prevention. *Communication Research Reports*, 28(4), 318–326. (Researchers explore the effects of message framing on females' decisions to receive a popular vaccine.)

Valkenburg, P. M., H.A. Semetko, and C.H. De Vreese. (1999). The effects of news frames on readers' thoughts and recall. *Communication Research*, 26(5), 550–569. (An experimental study that examines the effects of different frames on individuals' ability to recall information.)

Yocco, V.S. (2014). Framing effective messages to motivate your users. *Smashing Magazine* http://mng.bz/39m4. (A how-to guide on effectively framing communication.)

KEYWORDS: framing communication, framing effects, framing theory, gain frame, loss frame

## 7.8    Summary

- Framing communication involves setting the tone in which you want users to receive and interpret your message.
- Understanding and motivation are two key components you need to account for in framing communication.
- Your design accounts for understanding when you make sure your message is clear, relatable, and on the level of ability of users and potential users.
- Your design accounts for motivation when you provide users with clear calls to action that make sense in the context of the message.
- Creating a well-framed message involves a number of steps, including (1) identifying what you want to communicate, (2) interviewing users to determine how to meet their needs, (3) choosing a framing technique, (4) choosing your frame of communication, (5) creating your message, (6) testing your message, and (7) releasing your well-framed message.
- Framing techniques include artifact, contrast, metaphor, slogan, stories, spin, and tradition.
- Frames of communication include gain-based, loss-based, and value-based frames.

# Persuasion: the deadliest art

*8*

Samantha is looking online for more information to make a decision on purchasing a new car. She wants a car that's sporty yet safe. She has narrowed her choices and sits staring at the websites of the manufacturers of the last two options she's considering:

- Car brand X shows a generic picture of a car and a word wall describing the safety features and awards the car has won. Samantha gets distracted before she can make it to the paragraph describing the safety features and awards.
- Car brand Y features a prominent picture of the sporty model Samantha likes, along with emblems and banners of safety awards the car has received. When Samantha hovers over one of the emblems, a concise sentence

160

describing the award pops up. She happily loses the next hour of her life reading half a dozen articles about the car that the site links to, eventually deciding to make an appointment with her local dealer.

If Samantha would've stayed on the first car's website long enough, she would've read that it had received the most safety awards in its class for the last decade. But the first car never stood a chance for long-term consideration, thanks to the persuasive elements of the second car's website.

Persuasion (figure 8.1) is a process in which an individual encounters information meant to lead to the development of new attitudes, or the reinforcement of existing attitudes; for example, a public service announcement warning not to text and drive. Persuasion involves shaping or reinforcing an attitude. This is important because people strive to hold the correct attitude. Would you want to be wrong if you thought exercise was bad for your heart, and therefore chose not to engage in exercise on a regular basis? Similarly, you want to think smoking and drinking to excess is a bad thing for your body. This helps avoid behaviors that cause irreversible damage.

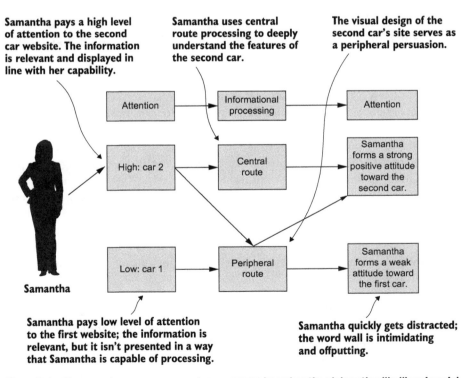

**Figure 8.1   How people process persuasive messages based on the elaboration likelihood model by Petty & Cacioppo, 1986**

This chapter will introduce you to the principle of persuasion. We'll explore the process that leads to a person becoming persuaded—or not persuaded—to use your product. You'll see how to craft a design that will address multiple aspects of persuasion. This chapter shows how your design can account for persuasion using two imaginary highways for processing information in the brain:

- The *central route*—where individuals pay close attention to information they consider important
- The *peripheral route*—where individuals pay less attention to the information, and more attention to environmental factors such as humor, fun pictures, or sex appeal of the message sender

## 8.1  Introduction

Persuasion is key to our everyday work as designers. The point of engaging in persuasion is for you to shape your users' attitudes toward your product, leading to the use of your product. Without persuasion, we aren't providing focus to our users.

> **NOTE**  Persuasion is a method of influence. Engaging in persuasion involves your design providing clear messages (through multiple media types) to users. Persuasion focuses on generating a new or reinforced attitude toward a product and its use, with the assumption that the attitude will generate the behavior.

We frequently engage in, and are subject to, persuasion. We ask our users to write a positive review if they've had a good experience with our product. Politicians ask us to vote for or against specific issues based on their ideology. Banks offer special financial incentives to conduct business with them. If we want to be good at persuasion, we need to know how the process works and when to use specific persuasive tactics. Otherwise, we risk alienating potential users with ineffective messages or persuasively designed experiences we deliver at the wrong time.

Persuasion is not a dark art, nor does it involve lying, cheating, or unethical dark patterns in your design. Persuasion is also difficult to accomplish. You face a number of obstacles in accomplishing your goal of persuading users to try your product. We've developed a number of mental defense mechanisms over the evolution of humanity that attempt to prevent others from persuading us. I'll cover these in this chapter as well.

### 8.1.1  Academic background

The Elaboration Likelihood Model (ELM) provides the template for this chapter's principle. Academic researchers Richard Petty and John Cacioppo developed the ELM in the early 1980s to explain how persuasive information forms or reinforces individuals' attitudes (which lead to behaviors). The prevailing logic at the time was that attitudes would form or shift based on the strength of an argument presented. The researchers speculated that many other factors exist that persuade people, besides the information they're presented with.

The researchers conducted studies presenting participants with numerous persuasive arguments, using a variety of medium to deliver them. For example, the researchers presented groups of participants with a persuasive essay about the need to take college exams. Participants also received a picture of the person researchers said wrote the essay. Some participants received a picture of a person rated more socially attractive (physically attractive and described to participants as having a good family background). The researchers found evidence that people were persuaded by attraction: statements made by people deemed more socially attractive were rated higher than similar statements attributed to less attractive people. Researchers also found that people rated recognizable sports and pop culture icons as being more credible than unknowns and that perceived credibility can contribute to increases in positive attitudes. (Participants receiving an essay attributed to a Princeton professor gave higher ratings than a group receiving the same essay attributed to a college student.)

Researchers conducted another study in which they gave advertisements about a new razor to two separate groups. One group thought the razor would be available for purchase in their local stores (more relevant), whereas researchers told the other group they wouldn't be able to have immediate access to the razor (less relevant). The group that thought they'd have access to the razor developed positive or negative attitudes toward the razor based on the strength of the argument in the ad. The group without access to the razor was more likely to form a positive attitude toward the razor based on secondary factors such as having a sports celebrity endorse the razor.

The ELM is one of the most highly cited models of persuasion. Although it comes from a background in marketing and communication, the ELM has widespread application beyond these fields. Research using the ELM provides evidence that you need to account for more than a strong message if you want to persuade users. We know that people will also pay attention to how you deliver the message as well as many other secondary factors.

## 8.2 Key concepts of persuasion

Researchers Petty and Cacioppo generated a model in 1986 (see the additional resources) describing how persuasion occurs in individuals. Their basic premise is that people encounter information (persuasive message), decide if they care about paying attention to the information (attention), and then process the information accordingly (route of processing). Researchers have used this model to explain and support findings from thousands of subsequent studies on the factors relevant to persuasion.

### 8.2.1 Determining if people pay attention: Capability and relevancy

Two factors will determine how much attention someone will give to a persuasive design or message:

- *Capability*—Do people have the ability to process the information they're receiving? Do they understand the issue and the argument you're presenting? It's unlikely a picture of a skunk will make someone who has never encountered or heard of a skunk associate it with the smell many of us who have encountered skunks do associate with it. You don't have the ability to understand what a skunk is if you've never encountered one in real life or by reading or watching TV.

- *Relevancy*—Is the issue meaningful or relevant to the individual encountering the persuasive message? Issue involvement is a key factor in motivating high levels of attention. If you don't own a smartphone, then you won't find much relevancy in a new smartphone calendar app. Conversely, if you're actively searching for a new smartphone calendar app, you're more likely to pay close attention to the information and experience of the new application.

### 8.2.2  *Central route processing*

Individuals mentally process information through what researchers call *central route processing* under conditions of high attention. Individuals process information based on the level of importance they assign based on capability and relevancy. People closely examine the information that they process in the central route of their brains. When people form attitudes through the central route, those attitudes become more permanent and harder to change than ones that people form under the peripheral route (section 8.2.3).

Emily is a huge fan of local sports. She regularly uses her smartphone and tablet to access information via topic-specific applications such as news, sports, and travel. Emily logs in one day to pay her Comcast bill and receives an offer to watch a video about a new local sports-focused application and enter a contest for a free iPad. Emily is very interested in the sports app. She's been searching for a suitable way to follow her favorite teams for quite a while (relevancy). She isn't that interested in winning the iPad—she already owns one—but the offer is a nice touch.

Emily pays close attention to the video advertising the new app because it's a product she might use every day. The video contains many screenshots and provides a link to download the app (capability). Emily realizes the app is missing a number of key functions she'd find useful: tracking individual teams, customizing alerts, and purchasing tickets in app. Emily forms a strong negative attitude toward the application. Later during conversation, Emily tells her fellow sports fan friends they should keep looking for a suitable sports app; the Comcast app just won't cut it.

To recap, Emily assigned a high level of *attention* to watching the video because

- She's interested in local sports teams (relevant).
- She regularly uses applications to access information (relevant).
- She has been searching for a suitable local sports app (relevant).
- The information was presented in an easy-to-manage video (capability).
- BONUS: She's already a Comcast customer and familiar with its products (capability).

Emily's high level of attention led to *central route processing* and her formation of a strong negative opinion, because the application is missing key features she needs. Emily is unlikely to change her mind about the app without strong convincing otherwise.

### 8.2.3   *Peripheral route processing*

Individuals mentally process information through the peripheral route under conditions of low attention.

Sharon is not a fan of her local sports teams. One day, she logs in to pay her Comcast bill and sees the message about entering a contest for a free iPad (figure 8.2). All she has to do to enter the contest is watch a video about their local sports app. Sharon doesn't care much about the local sports app, but decides she'll watch the video because she wants the opportunity to win the iPad. Sharon assigns low importance to the information related to the Comcast sports app.

Sharon watches the video while sending text messages to her friend about their evening plans. Happily, Sharon completes the iPad drawing entry that surfaces at the end of the video. Later that evening, Sharon's friends are talking about local sports and how hard it is to keep track of all the latest news and scores. Sharon recommends the Comcast sports app, even though she's never used it. She tells her friends it's probably a good way to monitor local sports teams. Sharon formed a positive attitude toward the Comcast app. She felt positive because the app allowed her to enter a contest to win something she wants.

Sharon assigned a low level of *attention* to watching the video because

- She isn't interested in local sports teams (relevant).
- She's more interested in the potential to win an iPad (relevant).
- She's distracted with texting her friend (relevancy).
- She lets the video play in her web browser (capability).

Sharon's low level of attention led to *peripheral route processing* and her formation of a weak positive opinion, because she was able to enter to win a free iPad. Sharon's attitude could easily change about the app in the future. A competing app might have a drawing for a prize she's even more interested in, for example, swaying Sharon to have a higher opinion of using that sports app.

**Figure 8.2   Giveaways and contests can encourage the formation of a positive attitude through peripheral route processing.**

## 8.3 *How to design for persuasion*

You should enjoy designing for persuasion. These elements will set your product apart. Your design should always take into consideration users that experience high and low levels of attention for your product. Additionally, an effectively designed product has the opportunity to move users along from low attention to high attention as they engage with your product. Let's learn more about designing to grab users' attention.

### 8.3.1 *Getting users to pay close attention*

Researchers have identified capability and relevancy as key features that cause high levels of attention.

#### USERS MUST BE CAPABLE OF USING YOUR DESIGN

Users must be capable of understanding the interactions and purpose of your design. Your design might directly address users' most important needs, but if they can't finish a workflow, they won't be using your product to meet their needs.

Squarespace (figure 8.3), the website-building platform, increases the capability of users and potential users through

- *Simple interactions*—Potential users are greeted with a simple homepage and the prominent call to action "Get Started."
- *Templates*—Users are immediately presented with templates and the ability to preview each template. Note they don't have to enter any information or engage in any other task before selecting a template. It couldn't be easier to start using a product than that. Users wishing to continue moving forward must then register. Squarespace organizes its content in a simple manner.

#### HOW TO DESIGN FOR CAPABILITY

Some of the ways you can design to increase users' capability include providing the following:

- *Logically organized content*—Present information within your product using labeling and navigation categories that you've tested with users.
- *Simple interactions*—Design for users to accomplish one clearly defined task at a time, with the ability to save and pick up where they left off.
- *Templates*—Most of your users aren't power users. A blank page is intimidating and users look to your product for guidance.
- *Contextual tool tips, manageable FAQs, and help documents*—Help your users learn quickly within the context of the activity they're engaged in. Don't make users navigate away from a workflow if they have a question.

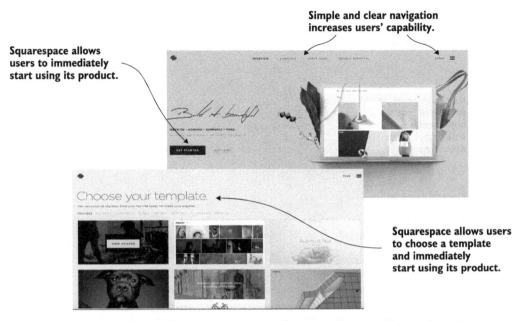

**Simple and clear navigation increases users' capability.**

**Squarespace allows users to immediately start using its product.**

**Squarespace allows users to choose a template and immediately start using its product.**

Figure 8.3  Squarespace provides simple interactions, clear calls to action, and templates to increase user capability.

### USERS NEED TO SEE THE RELEVANCY OF YOUR DESIGN

Users must understand your product's purpose and why it matters. If a user doesn't understand the purpose of your product, they won't know whether or not it's relevant. Medium (figure 8.4), the online blogging platform, creates immediate relevancy for users. Medium users want to do one of two major tasks: create a blog post or read a blog post. Medium immediately presents users with these options:

- Create a new post directly from the landing page.
- View recommended posts immediately from your feed.
- Click a trending tag to see related articles.
- Choose from top stories.
- Search for what you want to read.

### HOW TO DESIGN FOR RELEVANCY

You increase relevancy when your design is clear about what your product does, and how users can accomplish their goals with it. Your design should

- Display clear calls to action.
- Present users with one task at a time.
- Contain images and branding in line with user expectations for your product. (Don't have a bunch of cat videos available if your product is online banking.)

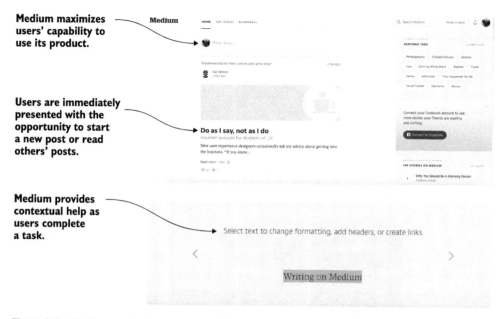

**Medium maximizes users' capability to use its product.**

**Users are immediately presented with the opportunity to start a new post or read others' posts.**

**Medium provides contextual help as users complete a task.**

**Figure 8.4    Medium makes the relevancy of its product immediately clear, allowing users to start a new post and read a blog post. Medium also addresses capability using contextual help while users create a new post.**

Keep in mind that your product can't be all things to all people. If your product is a tool for tracking the various types of beer users drink, recovering alcoholics and those leading a sober lifestyle truly have no use for your app. You need to accept when those situations occur, and focus your resources on audiences you can influence.

### 8.3.2    Designing for users' paying close attention

You have your users' attention—great job! Now comes the hard part. Once users begin processing information, it will be the quality of the argument or design that determines whether they gain a favorable attitude toward your product. Strong arguments create a positive attitude toward the topic; weak arguments create negative attitudes toward your product. This means you need to provide users with the information they need—a high-quality argument that your product is right for them—and you have to give them access to this information easily.

If your product is an e-commerce site or an application that helps users purchase goods and services, this means you should give users the ability to easily find what they're looking for. You do so with clear and logical navigation categories, accurate searching, relevant results filters, product comparison tools, and personalized account settings. Macy's (figure 8.5) provides users with a variety of filters to help manage search results on its site.

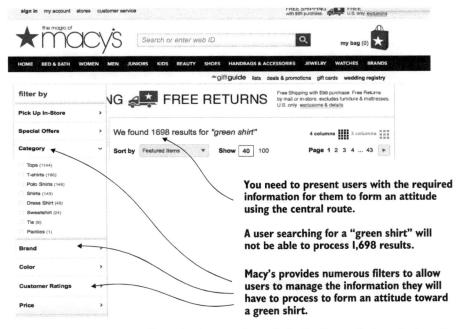

**Figure 8.5** Macy's provides filters that let users focus their attention on the important results of a search.

If your product is a game or a task-based application, your interactions need to unfold quickly and in line with users' expectations. Show and tell users about the meaningful features of your product. You should provide users with the critical information they need to get started immediately, and then continue to build their skills as they engage deeper with your product. Information overload is real, and it can kill users' interest in your product.

Your design should also avoid pointless or mistimed interruptions. For example, Walgreens (figure 8.6) presents a modal window asking users to complete a survey about their experience, impeding users' progress as they check out. If you ask users to take a survey about their experience at the same time they are trying to check out, they won't report positive experiences. Walgreens should initiate the modal on the confirmation screen after the purchase.

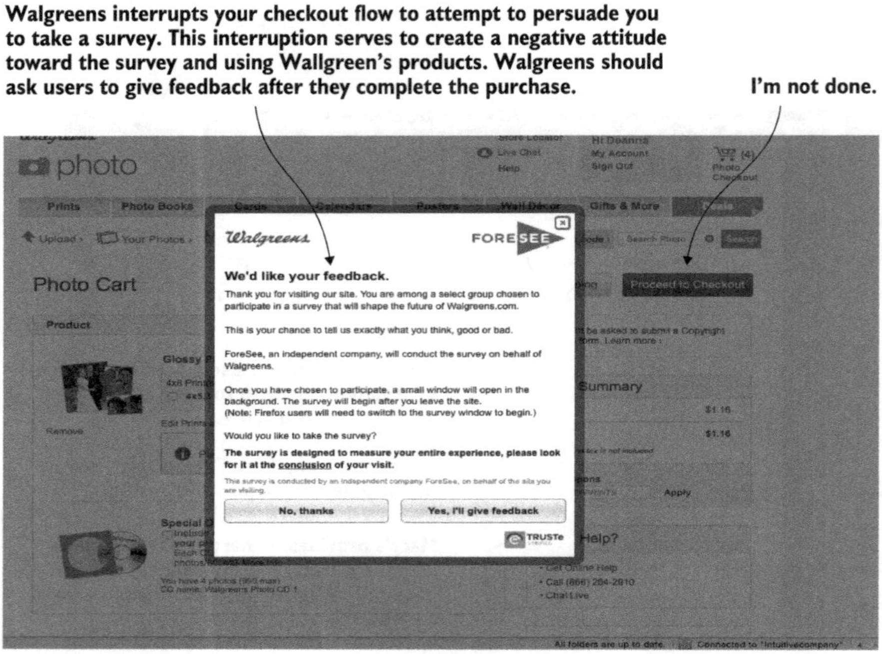

**Walgreens interrupts your checkout flow to attempt to persuade you to take a survey. This interruption serves to create a negative attitude toward the survey and using Wallgreen's products. Walgreens should ask users to give feedback after they complete the purchase.**

**I'm not done.**

**Figure 8.6    Walgreens interrupts users during important workflows. This prevents users from paying close attention to the products they're viewing, and possibly reduces purchases.**

#### HOW TO DESIGN FOR CENTRAL ROUTE PROCESSING

The most important point to remember is that the strength of your argument is what will lead to the formation and reinforcement of users' attitudes toward your product. Your design must contain and clearly present the information users need. Include elements such as

- A clear visual hierarchy highlighting important information
- Contextual help and tool tips—don't remove users from the experience to learn more
- Detailed product descriptions
- Jargon-free descriptions and instructions

- Product pictures and images that help tell the story of your site
- Relevant filters and sorting options

### 8.3.3 *Designing for users with low attention spans*

Your users aren't interested in paying close attention to the details of your product. Even if they are, now is the time to capitalize on well-placed elements of persuasion to transition your users from low attention to high attention with your product. Examples of these elements are fairly common online and in marketing throughout different mediums:

- *Affinity recommendations*—If users don't know what or why they'd use your product, they might use other people like themselves as a reference point.
- *Experts*—Don't know which X to use? Don't care? Just do what X does and use XX.
- *Humor*—People identify with humor, and remember when something is funny; spice up your tax preparation website with some wit, but don't overdo it.
- *Money*—Paying people, reducing or waiving fees, and not charging for a service facilitate the formation of a positive attitude through the peripheral route.
- *Music*—Playing familiar or catchy music can help users attach a positive attitude to your product.
- *Prizes*—People love to get something for nothing. Holding a contest or drawing is a good way to gain initial interest in trying your product through the peripheral route.
- *Rewards programs*—Go beyond the random prize and allow loyal users to earn perks and status. Present them with discounts and special opportunities based on their purchasing, searching, and viewing history.
- *Sex appeal*—Sex appeal is the romance novel cover of persuasion. It also works. I challenge you to think broadly in your use of sex appeal. Not everyone is attracted to the opposite sex. Not everyone is attracted to the same type of surface-level beauty. Can you create a more inclusive experience and use sex appeal at a level that the LGBTQ community would find appropriate? Can you mix the race, size, and shape of the humans you feature on your marketing materials? If not, it might be best to stick with images of cats.
- *Security*—Users know there are nefarious people looking to do unwholesome things with their data. You can convey a greater sense of security when you include third-party verification seals, date-stamped security test results, and jargon-free messages ensuring data encryption and security.
- *Status*—Users attach a higher value to something they perceive to be a status symbol, or a symbol of quality.
- *Visual appeal*—There's no doubt that effective visual design can persuade users.
- *Many additional techniques*—I've listed articles that explore many of these techniques in the additional resources.

## 8.4    *Talking the talk: Conversations about persuasion*

Your clients and peers will be familiar with many of the concepts (and the underlying logic) of the types of persuasion your design incorporates. Let's say your product is an application people can use to track the movies they've watched and ones they'd like to see in the future:

- *Attention*—"We know people will find our application useful. We need to make sure our design immediately shows them how and why they'll want to track movies. If we do this, they'll pay close attention to the features of the app to determine whether they want to download and use it."

- *Relevancy*—"Users will immediately see how the product applies to their interests. We list the top 10 movies currently in theaters and ask them to select the movies they've seen or would like to. From there, they begin the account creation process, and the movies they've already selected are prepopulated in their record."

- *Capability*—"We made the app as easy as possible for users to download. We placed QR codes on a number of movie posters. We made the app a free download, and we believe many users are already familiar with how to use the app store."

- *High attention*—"We want to encourage users to learn more about the app. We need to make it immediately clear how our product meets users' needs. We're presenting users with a description of the app and allowing them to compare the features with similar existing products. We believe our features are more valuable and easier to use than those of our competitors."

- *Navigation*—"We've restructured the navigation and subnavigation to reflect how users perceive the relationship between navigational categories (for example, film genres). This will reduce users' mental effort and increase their perception that your site efficiently meets their needs. We used feedback from interviews to inform how we restructured the navigation."

- *Low attention*—"We know some users will benefit from additional motivation to use our app. We have made a number of design enhancements to help promote use of our application to these types of users."

- *Loyalty*—"We're allowing users to track their spending on movie tickets or rentals. In turn, users will receive discounts for products and can eventually earn a free ticket to a movie of their choice. We foresee the cost offset by partnerships with movie theaters and distributors of products related to the various films we'll promote to users. We partnered with a major movie studio to feature our app on the web pages of a number of their new releases. Users will connect use of the app with an upcoming movie they want to see, and download the app for use."

- *Gamification*—"We've created a hierarchical system of titles people can earn based on the number of films they report viewing (for example, from 'Noob' to 'Film Critic'). Any messages or reviews users leave on the app reflect this status.

This should serve to motivate users to engage more with our app, earning a higher title than their peers do."

## 8.5 Case study: PayPal

PayPal is synonymous with sending and receiving money online. This didn't happen by accident. It happened with assistance from well-placed and persuasively designed features located throughout the product. Let's explore how PayPal appeals to users through both central and peripheral route processing.

### 8.5.1 Attention

Individuals tend to inherently pay attention to the topic PayPal deals with: money! PayPal has grown over time and is very relevant to users: most people have had the opportunity to send or receive money via PayPal. I was sending money to my landlord using PayPal in 2008, and my landlord was not at all tech savvy. Let's review how Pay-Pal's design takes advantage of both high and low attention when users are processing information.

#### CAPABILITY

PayPal addresses capability for both sending and receiving money (figure 8.7). PayPal

- Doesn't require users to create an account to send money
- Allows users to simply enter an email or phone number they want to send money to
- Doesn't charge users to send money or use its product for payment
- Allows users to connect an outside account to transfer received money

**Figure 8.7** PayPal's homepage addresses capability (Sign Up For Free) and relevancy (169 million others use it to shop).

Once users take advantage of the product to receive money, the process is almost as simple: link a checking or savings account and you can start receiving money from others.

**RELEVANCY**

PayPal is about money. Money is inherently relevant to most people. PayPal made strategic partnerships that allowed its product to become more relevant as the payment product recommended by eBay in the early 2000s when eBay was experiencing extreme popularity. eBay eventually purchased PayPal.

### 8.5.2    *High attention*

PayPal presents information that's clear and useful. PayPal facilitates users' deeper exploration of its product by allowing users to take advantages of certain components (such as making a payment) without requiring a deeper investment.

PayPal does the following:

- Provides access to relevant, role-based information, such as merchant versus customer versus billing someone (figure 8.8)
- Offers easily accessible contact information, FAQs, and how-to videos
- Explains use in an easy-to-understand, jargon-free manner
- Categorizes content in logical navigation categories
- Has easy-to-use workflows for sending a payment

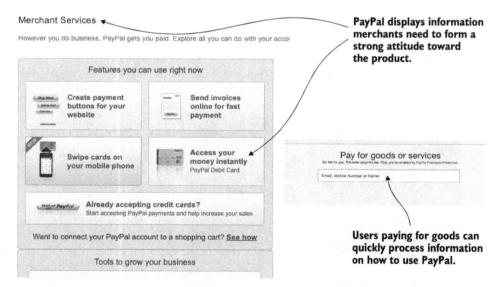

**Figure 8.8    PayPal presents information for merchants and those sending money to easily understand how the product will meet their needs.**

### 8.5.3   Low attention

PayPal has successfully implemented a number of features that appeal to users with low attention to its product initially, including

- Aligning its brand with eBay increased users' perception (expertise)
- Offering users discounts at specific merchants (figure 8.9) (loyalty/reward)
- Including its logo along with other more traditional, trusted payment merchants such as MasterCard and Visa (status and trust)
- Having a straightforward fee system (money)
- Allowing free use of sending money (money)
- Including PayPal branded buttons for making a payment (visual design)

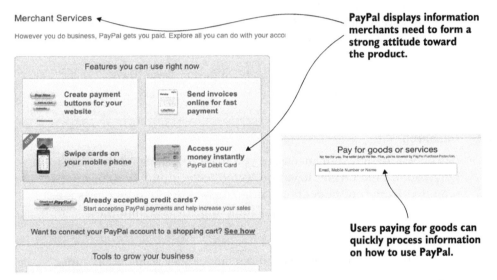

**Figure 8.9**   PayPal presents information for merchants and those sending money to easily understand how the product will meet their needs.

## 8.6   End-of-chapter exercise: Sexy chocolate bar persuasive design activity

Imagine you're tasked with designing material for a persuasive digital marketing campaign for the Sexy Chocolate Bar Co.'s flagship product—a bar of dark chocolate. You'll be focusing your campaign on persuading customers from the following personas. At a minimum, you have to give the product a name and design the outer wrapper. You're free to go beyond this and develop a web page, poster, slogan, or other marketing material. You can share your answers and provide feedback on the Manning Publications forum here: https://forums.manning.com/forums/design-for-the-mind.

### 8.6.1    *Personas*

Choose at least one of the following personas to design for:

- A middle-aged male with no sense of smell and who is color blind
- A teenage boy who's allergic to chocolate and the leader of his group of friends
- A 45-year-old man who is on a strict diet and is a member of Weight Watchers
- An elderly lady with 35 cats who loves knitting
- The kids from the *Breakfast Club* movie
- Edward Scissorhands
- An escaped convict who was serving time for grand theft auto
- The cast of *Duck Dynasty*
- Aliens from Mars
- A 35-year-old single mother working in the Sexy Chocolate Bar Co.'s factory
- A 50-year-old man addicted to gambling
- A young couple who has just purchased their first house and has little disposable income
- A middle-aged cacao (cocoa) bean farmer from Brazil
- A young woman who has recently won the lottery
- A legally blind chocolate lover

### 8.6.2    *Research*

Before you design your materials, you need to gather information from your target population. Pretend you have conducted focus groups and/or interviews with representatives from your target population. Answer the following questions:

1  What does your target population value or find important?

2  What are some interests and hobbies of your target population?

3  What motivates their purchasing behaviors?

4  What are some challenges you face in persuading your target population to purchase chocolate bars?

5  What are some strategies you might consider to persuade your target population to purchase chocolate bars?

**Okay! Now design your marketing materials and then respond to the following:**

Briefly explain how the campaign you've designed addresses some of the elements of persuasive communication that were discussed in this chapter.

- How does your design address central route processing?
- How does your design address peripheral route processing?

## 8.7  *Additional resources*

Angst, C.M., and R. Agarwal. (2009). Adoption of electronic health records in the presence of privacy concerns: The elaboration likelihood model and individual persuasion. *MIS Quarterly*, 33(2), 339–370. (An article using the elaboration likelihood model to explain why people are [or are not] in favor of electronic health records.)

Chen, S.H., and K.P. Lee. (2008). The role of personality traits and perceived values in persuasion: An elaboration likelihood model perspective on online shopping. *Social Behavior and Personality: An International Journal*, 36(10), 1379–1399. (Researchers use the elaboration likelihood model to examine persuasion in e-commerce.)

Petty, R.E., and J.T. Cacioppo. (1984). Source factors and the elaboration likelihood model of persuasion. *Advances in Consumer Research*, 11(1), 668–672. (Petty and Cacioppo discuss the effect of source factors such as attractiveness and credibility on persuasion.)

—————————. (1986). *The elaboration likelihood model of persuasion.* New York: Springer. (Petty and Cacioppo introduce the elaboration likelihood model and their research supporting the components of the model.)

SanJosé-Cabezudo, R., A.M. Gutiérrez-Arranz, and J. Gutiérrez-Cillán. (2009). The combined influence of central and peripheral routes in the online persuasion process. *CyberPsychology & Behavior*, 12(3), 299–308. (Researchers examine an updated perspective of the elaboration likelihood model in order to account for online persuasion.)

Tam, K.Y., and S.Y. Ho. (2005). Web personalization as a persuasion strategy: An elaboration likelihood model perspective. *Information Systems Research*, 16(3), 271–291. (Researchers examine the role of website personalization in order to influence users.)

KEYWORDS: central route, dual process theory, Elaboration Likelihood Model (ELM), peripheral route, persuasion

## 8.8  *Summary*

- Attention, information processing, and attitude are the key components of the principle of persuasion.
- Your users will pay close attention to your design when you show them how your product is relevant to their life or the problem at hand.

- High levels of attention lead to users processing information through the central route.

- Attitudes formed through central route processing are based on the strength of an argument.

- Your design can create a strong argument by providing accurate and easy-to-process information; allowing users to filter and sort information; and using clear, jargon-free language.

- Attitudes formed through central route processing tend to be strongly held and hard to change.

- Users incapable of processing your product's design, or who fail to see the relevancy of your product, will process information through the peripheral route.

- Your design can account for peripheral route processing by including elements such as affinity recommendations, money, sex appeal, rewards, and visual appeal.

# Part 4

## User experience design: putting it all together

This final part of the book will provide a review of the principles and actionable next steps for applying what you've learned to your practice.

Chapter 9 presents a case study that will allow you to apply components of each of the principles we've covered. You'll see an example of how to think through the use of psychology from the conception of an idea, through its implementation. You'll also understand that these principles allow flexibility in how they're used. There's no one-size-fits-all approach to any of the principles. You can pick and choose how to apply them, in the way that best suits your product and its users.

Chapter 10 provides the information you need to continue moving forward with what you've learned. You'll see how you might account for psychological principles over all phases of a design project. I'll give you insight into which principles might be best for your product, and you'll learn some common user experience research methods you should use to help inform your design. Finally, I'll provide methods to measure the impact of incorporating principles of psychology into the design of your product.

# Case study: KidTech Design Co.'s Good Choice app

**This chapter covers**

- Using pieces of multiple psychological principles for one project
- Applying the principles of psychology we've covered
- Using psychological principles with other UX design practices

We've now discussed seven principles of psychology you can immediately start to account for in your design to increase use and usability. This chapter provides a fictitious case study of a smartphone application in which the design team incorporated all or some components of many of the principles we have covered. The case study asks you to provide insight into what decisions you'd make, and then highlights how the KidTech team incorporated the principles.

## 9.1   Introduction

KidTech Design Co. is a startup composed of three partners: Maxwell the researcher, Emily the content strategist and project manager, and Eleanor, the UX designer. All three split front- and back-end coding duties.

KidTech received funding from a venture capitalist to build "Good Choice," a decision-making application for children between the ages of 12 and 18. Parents and children download the app to their smartphone or tablet. Children then use the app to assist in making decisions without their parents present. If a child wants to go over to her friend's house after school, she can consult the app to see whether it's a "good choice." The app will walk the user through a series of questions (for example, do you have homework tonight?) to determine if what the user is asking to do is a good choice based on an algorithm that also examines data from past choices. The app allows parents to select settings to make sure the application meets their needs. The parent can require they have final say in whether a decision is a "good choice" by receiving a notification that they have to respond to from their smartphone or tablet.

Although the app serves a functional purpose—to help parents and children develop a deeper trust around doing the right thing—the app also serves to facilitate a conversation with children on the importance of developing good decision-making skills—something they'll value as they transition into adulthood. I'll fill in the remaining details about the app as the chapter unfolds.

## 9.2    *Using psychology to justify an idea*

KidTech realizes designers should identify and understand the psychological principles underlying why users are likely to need their product. You strengthen your argument in favor of your idea when you can support it with psychology. We've covered principles of psychology you can use to help inform the initial design of your product. Imagine KidTech asks you to write up a brief statement on how the app will appeal to the psychology of users to include in their business case.

### 9.2.1    *How would you use psychology to justify the Good Choice app?*

Write a few sentences on how you'd use one or more of the principles of psychology from this book to justify the need for the Good Choice app:

- Which principle(s) do you think provide a good justification for the application?
- Why?
- What specific pieces of the principle(s) would you discuss?
- How would you extend the principle(s) into the actual design of the app?

### 9.2.2    *How KidTech used psychology to justify the Good Choice app: Planned behavior*

The KidTech team used the concepts from the principle of planned behavior (chapter 2) to inform the creation of their product. KidTech's intention was to create an application that users would plan to use, as well as one that would assist children in making planned decisions.

The KidTech team discussed how their idea would meet users' needs for each of the three concepts before developing their pitch for funding. KidTech presented the following justifications for how the Good Choice app aligned with users' psychology through the principle of planned behavior.

### BEHAVIOR BELIEFS

Most parents believe having children make informed decisions is a good thing. They want to promote the behavior of having their child understand the consequences of a decision. Most children think making decisions autonomously is a good thing. They want to engage in this behavior as soon as possible. Also, most people want to make good decisions, ones that will leave them in a better place than they were before. The application can be a tool to assist in both large and small decisions.

### NORMATIVE BELIEFS

In most societies and mainstream social circles, a child asking an adult for permission to engage in an activity is normal behavior. Smartphone and tablet application use is continuing to increase among youthful populations. Using a smartphone application is considered a social norm among most age groups in First World nations.

### CONTROL BELIEFS

The application takes advantage of extending current control beliefs. Parents believe they should have control over the decision-making of their children, and children are usually aware that their parents have the final say in what they do. The application serves to extend the control of parents by engaging with a smartphone app. The app also increases children's perceptions of control. It seems easier to consult an app on their phone about whether a decision is a good choice and then make the decision rather than consult a parent. People want to be in control over the outcome of their decisions as well. The app provides greater insight into whether users' choices are likely to lead to a better outcome based on whether the decision is a "good choice."

### 9.2.3 *How KidTech extended planned behavior into the design of their product*

KidTech was able to extend the components of the principle of planned behavior into the Good Choice app design.

### BEHAVIOR BELIEFS

The app rewards children for making "good choices." They earn points redeemable for sponsor-provided gift cards. Parents must approve the accrual of points for each decision by confirming that the child followed through with the good choice.

### NORMATIVE BELIEFS

The app incorporates features that reinforce the fact that using an app to assist in decision-making is a socially acceptable behavior. This includes areas where users can post ideas about things like

- How they've used the app to increase trust between parents and children
- Unique group activities
- Ideas other users have suggested
- Testimonials from a variety of users

### CONTROL BELIEFS

Parents select the settings of the app for approving decisions. Parents can select options requiring preapproval of all decisions marked as a "good choice" or allow the app to have the final say in certain user-defined choices, such as visiting preapproved friends after school. Parents receive a notice of all activity and are given time to review a decision that the app has determined will be a "good choice." These same features allow child users to develop a greater sense of control over their decision-making. As children engage in more good choices, they'll feel empowered over their ability to make positive decisions. They'll also know that their parents are aware of the good decisions they're making.

## 9.3   *Nervous parents and uncertain outcomes*

KidTech wanted their application to be simple and fun to use. They didn't want users thinking too hard about whether the app was beneficial to their lives. Maxwell conducted interviews and found parents felt that letting their child use the application would have uncertain outcomes. Application features would need to reassure parents they were making a good decision to let their child use the app.

### 9.3.1   *How would you reassure parents and address uncertainty?*

As an exercise, write a few sentences on how you'd use one or more of the principles of psychology to reassure users the Good Choice app will help them accomplish their goals. Also, how would you reduce users' uncertainty about the decisions they make—both the decision to use the app *and* the decisions they use the app to make?

- Which principle(s) do you think provide guidance on ways to reassure users?
- Why?
- How would you include the principle(s) in your design?
- What UI elements might reassure users according to the principle(s)?
- How might you use the principle(s) to address user uncertainty?
- What UI elements support users' use and reuse of apps?
- How might you design the app to increase certainty and trust with users?

### 9.3.2   *How KidTech addressed reassuring parents and uncertainty*

KidTech designed features to address two components of risky decisions and mental shortcuts (chapter 3): loss aversion and escalation of commitment.

#### LOSS AVERSION

Maxwell found that parents want to start allowing their growing children to make decisions, but they don't want to lose control over the final say in those decisions. Parents also stated their children don't want to lose their privileges, so they try to make good decisions.

Maxwell reported that the application naturally takes advantage of loss aversion (section 3.2.3), and marketing of the product should clearly state this benefit. Maxwell also recommended settings for users to set the level of tolerance for loss—for example, being grounded—if the user makes a decision that's considered a bad decision. Parents and children would agree on the set punishment for making a particular decision. The app might advise a child not to go to her friend's house, reminding them that they got in trouble the last time they made that decision in a similar situation. The child then might opt to make the bad decision and take the consequence of being grounded, if the parent has agreed to allow that setting.

#### ESCALATION OF COMMITMENT

Escalation of commitment (section 3.3.6) involves having users invest time in using your product. Maxwell's research found that parents want to feel a connection with the technology and their children. Parents likely to use the application want it to enhance their relationship with their child, and they want to feel loyalty toward the application if it does what it's meant to. KidTech addressed escalation of commitment in two ways:

- The app shows users how many decisions they've made and the percentage of good versus bad outcomes. Showing users how frequently they use the app is a reminder of the time and effort they've invested in the app and of the past decisions they've made. Parents can discuss these decisions with children, and the application will allow them to record an audio, video, or written reflection.
- Users earn points that can only be redeemed through the app; the more decisions users make, the more points they get (particularly for good decisions); also, the points are only redeemable through the app for gift cards from sponsor companies, meaning users will continue using the app if they want to redeem their points. Both parents and children earn points, thus creating deeper commitment from both user types.

## 9.4 *Making it social*

Maxwell's research uncovered that child users want to share what they're doing over social media, particularly if it involves having fun with other friends. Parents have some concern over their children sharing their decisions publicly, but they'd also like to know what other parents are allowing their children to do.

### 9.4.1 *How would you make the Good Choice app social?*

Write a few sentences on how you'd use one or more of the principles of psychology to strategically make the Good Choice app social. Think about how you can increase use and harness the power of positive reviews and word-of-mouth recommendations:

- Which principle(s) do you think provide guidance on ways to create meaningful social experience?
- Why?
- How would you include the principle(s) in your design?
- What UI elements would facilitate social interactions through the app, according to the principle(s)?
- What social aspects of making decisions could you include in your design?

- When would you present users with opportunities to engage each other socially?

### 9.4.2  *How KidTech made the app social*

KidTech used the principle of social influence to ensure that they address the app's social experiences meaningfully.

#### SOCIAL INFLUENCE

The Good Choice app extended social norms covered in section 9.2.2 and incorporated additional elements of social influence (chapter 6).

Emily the content strategist is also a social media wiz. She advocated including a number of features to address users creating a social identity with the application, and using social influence:

- Users over the age of 13 have the ability to share their decisions and the outcomes over social media.

  The application allows users to generate tweets or Facebook posts such as "I just used Good Choice to get permission to eat dessert." These tweets serve to facilitate the potential for other children who follow users on social media to find out more about the application. Users can also post whether their decision was a "good choice" or a "bad choice" based on the outcome.

- Good Choice presents users with the ability to rate and write a recommendation for the app directly from the app.

  The timing of asking for a review is strategic—once users have made three good choices in a row. These users are more likely to experience satisfaction with the application.

Emily took the lead in addressing social identity issues by setting up separate Facebook, Twitter, and other social media accounts for parent users and child users. Users will develop stronger social ties by identifying which group they belong to (child or parent) and joining that group on social media.

Good Choice allows users to form groups to use the app to obtain permission. Again, this allows social identity to develop among app users—more children would want to use the app if they're part of a group asking their parents for permission through the application.

The application provides users with a Facebook-style newsfeed showing what choices their connections have made, as well as what the outcome was (good choice/ bad choice). Users see the choices their friends have made, such as attending a sports event or visiting a friend.

## 9.5  *Speaking clearly to users*

KidTech realized the importance of consistent communication with users and potential users. They needed to develop a communication plan for marketing the app and for communicating to users within the app.

### 9.5.1 *How would you recommend KidTech talk to users?*

Write a few sentences on how you'd use one or more of the principles of psychology to design communication to users within the app and marketing to potential users. Think about your audience and which principles provide guidance on communication:

- Which principle(s) provide guidance on ways to create meaningful communication with Good Choice app users and potential users?
- Why?
- How would you use principles of psychology to address communicating with users (in-app communication)?
- How would you use principles of psychology to address communicating with potential users?
- Use this space to write out some messages you'd present to users in-app. At what point would you surface these messages?
- Use this space to write out some of the messages you'd present to potential users to convince them to try the app.

### 9.5.2 *How KidTech designed their communication strategy*

KidTech used the information from interviews with potential users to determine the frames of communication (chapter 7) used within the application, and when talking about the application in marketing and other material.

#### MESSAGES FRAMED FOR CHILD USERS

KidTech framed communication to child users (ages 13 and up) with trust-based value frames and altruistic value frames. They also used pictures of children engaged in activities (and user-uploaded pictures) to help effectively frame the messages.

Examples of KidTech's messages to child users include

- You'll gain the trust of your parents when you use the Good Choice app with them (Trust).
- Making good choices increases your chance to gain independence (Trust).
- Your decisions can improve the situation for others as well (Altruistic).
- If the world had more decision makers like you, it'd be a better place (Altruistic).

#### MESSAGES FRAMED FOR PARENT USERS

Parents receive trust-framed messages and parental-framed messages while using the Good Choice app:

- You'll gain trust in your child's decisions when you use the Good Choice app (Trust).
- Good Choice allows you to empower your children to make the right choices (Trust and Parental).
- Decision-making is a critical skill for your child to develop (Parental).
- Good Choice app is your partner in turning your teen into a responsible adult (Parental).

## 9.6    Long-term engagement

KidTech realized the true value of their app was in long-term use. Parents will only learn to trust their children over time and over a series of good decisions. Children will only develop the skills they need to make good decisions through practice. KidTech reviewed their design to identify opportunities to make sure they're including design elements that facilitate long-term engagement informed by principles of psychology.

### 9.6.1    How would you make users want to keep using the app?

Write a few sentences on how you'd use one or more of the principles of psychology to ensure users want to continue using the app in the long term:

- Which principle(s) provide guidance on ways to create meaningful communication with Good Choice app users and potential users?
- Why?
- What features could you include to facilitate frequent engagement?
- How might principles of psychology inform your marketing and promotion of the app once users have registered?

### 9.6.2    How KidTech facilitated long-term use of the app

KidTech focused on the principle of influence (chapter 5) to facilitate long-term use of the Good Choice app.

#### COMMITMENT AND CONSISTENCY

The Good Choice app promotes commitment and consistency (section 5.2.2) from adult and child users.

The app asks adult users to commit to using the app for a specific number of decisions. They receive bonus loyalty points if they reach this number within a specific period. Adults input the types of decisions they're comfortable having their child use the app to facilitate (such as whether to go to a friend's house, the type of snack to eat after school, or what purchases to make with their allowance).

The app asks child users to check a box that they agree to the following statement: I'll use the Good Choice app to make decisions (about or when):

- My parent/guardian agrees that we can use the app.
- Additional statements that are populated based on parents' responses.

#### VISUAL INFLUENCE

KidTech uses visual influence (section 5.3.4) to demonstrate trust and power throughout the app.

#### TRUST

KidTech's visual design encourages user trust by displaying

- The secure, logged-in status of the user
- Images of users engaged in activities
- Testimonials from parents and children

They also allow users to modify what other users can see (for example, blocking their feed from others).

**POWER**

The Good Choice app conveys power through visual design by allowing users to customize the look of the dashboard and workflows. The app

- Presents users with clear pictures and proportional white space to facilitate the task of using the application
- Utilizes familiar icons
- Uses Helvetica and other sans-serif fonts meant to convey professionalism

**RECIPROCITY**

KidTech attempts to create a sense of reciprocity (sections 5.2.1 and 5.3.1) in users. KidTech gives users 500 loyalty points for creating an account online. This is enough for parents and children to redeem for a gift card from the loyalty store. Users earn another 500 points when they use the app to make their first good decision.

## 9.7 Low use of app after download

KidTech wasn't pleased with use of their app after its release. They were satisfied with the number of app downloads and accounts registered, but they found users weren't using the app to help make decisions as frequently as expected.

### 9.7.1 How would you help KidTech increase use after download?

Write a few sentences on how you'd use one or more of the principles of psychology to make recommendations to KidTech for moving users from downloading the app to using it as well:

- How would you find out more information on why use of the Good Choice app isn't as high as expected?
- Which principle(s) might explain why users aren't fully engaged with the app?
- What elements of the UI would you focus on increasing the use of the app after download?
- What features or functionality of the app would you recommend adding, removing, or tweaking?

### 9.7.2 How KidTech addressed increasing use after download

KidTech needed deep information on use of the app over time. Maxwell designed a diary study to collect data to determine what users did with the app after downloading it.

**MOTIVATION, ABILITY, AND TRIGGER (CHAPTER 4)**

KidTech's diary study found the app wasn't presenting users with the trigger (section 4.2.3) to make a decision at the correct time. Users wanted to record their potential choices but put off making the decision until later in the day. For example, users would open the app in the morning to check out what other decisions their friends were making, or because someone would ask them to do something (motivation; section 4.2.1). This was the point when the app would ask users if they wanted to make a choice (trigger). But this wasn't when users wanted to lock in their decision (ability; section 4.2.2).

KidTech deigned an update to include the ability for users to schedule a choice. Now users could open the app in the morning, and throughout the day, to enter potential choices. They'd then have the option to schedule their decision (trigger) for any time in the future. For example, a user could enter the potential choices of "hang out with friends at a restaurant after school" and "go to a football game with friends" first thing in the morning. Next, they could schedule the app to remind them to "Make the choice" later that day.

KidTech's follow-up research found that users had significantly increased making decisions with the app, mostly due to the ability to create decisions at one point and schedule them with a reminder trigger to make the decision at a later point.

## 9.8    *A closer look at persuasion*

The Good Choice app contains a number of design elements applying the principle of persuasion introduced in chapter 8. Let's break down the app using this principle.

### 9.8.1    *How do you think the Good Choice app addresses the principle of persuasion from chapter 8?*

- How does the app address relevancy to promote central route processing?
- How does the app address the ability to promote central route processing?
- How does the app meet users' informational needs during central route processing?
- What additional design recommendations would you make to facilitate central route processing?
- How does the app apply persuasive elements for users going through peripheral route processing?
- What additional design recommendations would you make to facilitate peripheral route processing?

### 9.8.2    *How KidTech's app addresses the principle of persuasion from chapter 8*

KidTech incorporated the principle of persuasion throughout the conceptualization and design of the app.

#### RELEVANCY AND ABILITY

The app addresses both relevancy and ability:

- The purpose of the app is clear: help users make good choices (relevancy). Potential users will see that the app addresses something that's important to their lives; decision-making is a key skill most families with teenagers need to address. The app's design doesn't distract users with other tasks or features; the focus is on decision-making and improving trust between parents and children.

- The app redesign (section 9.7.2) presents users with critical options upon launch and allows users to schedule decisions and decision reminders (ability). KidTech realized that users wanted to immediately engage in the task of making a choice or scheduling a choice. Presenting users with these options first increased their ability to use the app.

**HIGH ATTENTION**

The app meets users' information needs when they have high attention. It has clearly labeled fields requiring users to enter information for the decision. Child users answer the following:

- What is the choice?
- What are the options?
- What do you need to make the choice?
- When do you need to decide?
- What decision would you like to make?
- Who else is involved in the decision?
- Who else is involved in each choice?

Parent users answer the following:

- Do you have questions about each choice?
- What would you like the child to choose?
- Why would you like the child to choose this option?
- What are the potential consequences of a bad choice?
- What are the potential consequences of a good choice?

Additionally:

- Parents and children can message each other through the app to get more details about decision requests.
- The app provides a blueprint for building trust. For example, child users should make 10 smaller good decisions before asking about a bigger decision.
- The app allows users to categorize the decisions they make and view others' decisions by category.

**LOW ATTENTION**

The app meets users' information needs when they have low attention:

- Pictures are used to facilitate trust between parents and children, as the pictures suggest children are engaging in positive activities approved through the app.
- The loyalty points program persuades users to use the app in order to earn and spend loyalty points.
- The app allows user personalization of content and pictures.

## 9.9    *Talking the talk: Conversations about psychological principles*

KidTech used each principle in a straightforward way. The KidTech team can easily communicate these decisions to others:

- *Planned behavior*—"We've created an application that taps into the positive belief that building trust between adults and teenage children is good."
- *Risky decisions*—"We tap into child users' desires not to lose privileges and parents' desire not to lose control over their children."
- *Social influence*—"Child users are able to see what their friends and others are doing, and parents can see what their peers are allowing children to do."
- *Framing*—"We communicate with users in a way that establishes trust with the application and trust between adults and children."
- *Influence*—"Users will continue using our app as they earn points redeemable for gift cards at popular retailers."
- *Motivation, ability, and trigger*—"We addressed users' concerns over the app asking them to request a decision too early. The app now presents users with the option for a decision request at the appropriate time they designate."
- *Persuasion*—"Users will pay close attention to the information because this is a topic that's important to them. We clearly identify the purpose of the app from our initial marketing efforts, through the completion of making a decision."

## 9.10    *End-of-chapter exercise: Critique KidTech*

We've reviewed how KidTech addressed each principle covered in this book in their design. Now's your chance to critique their work. You can share your answers to the following questions and provide feedback on the Manning Publications forum at https://forums.manning.com/forums/design-for-the-mind:

How would you have addressed the following psychological principles differently if you'd designed the app?

- Planned behavior
- Risky decisions and mental shortcuts
- Motivation, ability, and trigger
- Influence
- Social identity and social influence
- Framing communication
- Persuasion
- What additional opportunities to address the principles did KidTech miss?
- Which principles complement each other the best? Why?

- What information would you include on a parent-view dashboard? Feel free to sketch out a design here.


- What information would you include on a child-view dashboard? Feel free to sketch out a design here.


## 9.11 Summary

- KidTech's app is an example of using the principles of psychology to help drive a project's design decisions from start to finish.
- KidTech understands the users they're designing for; user research is critical to gain that understanding.
- KidTech used the principle of planned behavior to make the business case for the need for the Good Choice app.
- The Good Choice app addresses loss aversion and escalation of commitment to reassure parents and reduce users' uncertainty.
- KidTech made the app social, allowing users to share their decisions with others and form groups. Users can also easily rate the app directly within the app.
- KidTech framed messages using altruism, parental, and trust frames. They used research with users to select these frames.
- KidTech used a number of concepts from the principle of influence to facilitate long-term use of the app: commitment and consistency, visual influence, trust, power, and reciprocity.
- KidTech used the principle of motivation, ability, and trigger to address lower than expected use of the app. They adjusted when the app presented users with the trigger to make a decision. They also increased users' ability to make a decision at the appropriate time by letting them schedule times to make a choice in the future.
- The Good Choice app addresses the principle of persuasion in a number of ways. Users see the relevancy of the app to their lives (making good choices) and the redesign of the app increased that ability by presenting relevant tasks immediately.
- The Good Choice app facilitates central route processing by presenting clearly labeled fields and by asking for relevant information based on user types. The app also provides users with a way to communicate more information to each other through the app.

- The Good Choice app facilitates peripheral route processing through the use of pictures, allowing users to earn loyalty points and allowing personalization.
- KidTech doesn't need to address every element of every principle to successfully use the principle.
- KidTech justified design updates and changes using principles of psychology.
- KidTech can easily discuss the inclusion of principles of psychology in their design.

# The next step: getting up and running

**This chapter covers**

- Identifying the role of psychological concepts in UX design
- Choosing the right principle(s) for your design
- Using common UX research methods
- Measuring the impact of incorporating psychology into your design

We've covered a lot of information in this book. This chapter discusses incorporating concepts from the book into your design process. Your understanding of psychology will help reduce the noise distracting you from focusing on effective design components. Your knowledge of how to account for psychological principles will ensure you design interactions that allow you to meet your goals.

You're probably aware that when thinking about the design process as a whole, you have to take a lot of factors into account. I've mentioned a number of things not covered in depth in this book—particularly research—that are critical for successful design. This chapter clarifies any outstanding questions on how the psychological principles fit into the process. I'll also cover what methods researchers use to gather data, in conjunction with the knowledge we have from psychology, to effectively design for the human mind.

## 10.1   *Part of the whole*

I've argued that knowledge of psychological principles is critical for effective and efficient design, which is mandatory for anyone engaging in UX design. You should incorporate psychology as part of the greater process you undertake during conceptualization, design, and redesign of a product. Your use of psychology should exist alongside conducting research with users and potential users, wireframing your concepts, testing and iterating on your design, and more. I don't believe one part of the process is more important than another. Clearly, the final design is what people see. What's less clear to users is how you arrived at your final design.

I'm not in favor of overly prescriptive approaches to design. I believe designers and design teams should have their own way of doing things. With that understanding, I'm providing the following guidance for four high-level phases so you can include principles of psychology into your design process.

### 10.1.1   *Phase 1: Idea conceptualization*

Phase 1 involves the creation of the idea or problem you're trying to solve through design. With your design team, determine how your idea will address key psychological principles and which ones support your concept. You strengthen your argument for funding or for a bigger budget from your supervisor when you're able to explain how your product will meet basic human needs and wants. You also set the stage for better focus during subsequent stages of design.

Chapter 9 highlighted how KidTech included planned behavior in conceptualizing the idea for its product. KidTech developers included psychological principles as an explicit part of conceptualizing their idea. They mapped how their design would address these principles and increase the likelihood of adoption. This map provided KidTech with the ability to speak clearly to others about their idea. The company's principals were also able to use a common language with each other when discussing their idea.

Section 10.2 will help you identify the most useful psychological principles to start with related to your idea. You should have a solid argument for the psychological reasoning before your idea ever hits the ground running. You must understand why your potential users would want to adopt your product; there will always be psychological reasons for this.

### 10.1.2   *Phase 2: Design conceptualization*

Once you conceptualize your idea and determine the psychological principles your product will address, you begin the process of designing. Designers usually begin wireframing at this time—creating black-and-white rough sketches of their design concept.

KidTech continued with the planned behavior elements and made critical design decisions based on the assumption of how their users viewed the concepts of planned behavior. For example, the developers assumed it was important to include design features highlighting the social norm of children making good decisions and involving parents in decision making. This was a direct outcome of including planned behavior in their idea conceptualization.

KidTech's use of planned behavior as a framework allowed them to efficiently examine potential components of its design through the lens of whether or not they contributed to meeting the various principles.

KidTech made additional design decisions using the remaining concepts we've covered. These were easier decisions supported by psychology and testing/observation (research). Feel free to dabble in multiple principles and only use the elements of a principle that work for you and your design.

You should produce visual concepts of your initial design and show different user types and workflows as the outcome of the design conceptualization phase.

### 10.1.3 *Phase 3: Design iteration*

Most good designs go through an iterative process where design features are tested, tweaked, and retested. I suggest including usability testing to inform the process of iteration. Users and potential users will find design issues that will save you time and money if you address them before finalizing your design and going to market. You can test your simple black-and-white wireframes or fully fleshed-out prototypes with aesthetic and branding elements in place.

I recommend testing your designs for their ability to address the psychological principles you've designed for. You might identify additional opportunities to incorporate minor features that address usability issues, as well as opportunities to make your product's design more persuasive to potential users. You should continue addressing these features and updates until you're ready to ship your product.

### 10.1.4 *Phase 4: Post shipment*

You shouldn't rest once you've shipped your design. Your product is likely to encounter more use cases than you imagined once it's user-accessible. These cases can inform future design updates and future products. You should actively collect data from your users, as well as analytical data on use of your design. You want to use analytics to determine the following:

- Which areas do users navigate to most frequently?
- Which areas do users navigate to least frequently?
- Where do users spend the most time?
- What sites are sending users to your site?
- What terms are users searching for to find your site?
- How often do users start and successfully complete tasks?
- How often do users start and successfully complete tasks?

You can use data from these questions to understand where you're successful and where you can improve.

Imagine you design a carpet-selling website with an accurate carpet size–estimating calculator. Your analytics show fewer than one out of every five users navigates to this tool. Additionally, you find that one of the most frequently asked questions to customer service involves how to estimate the size of your carpet. You need to look closer at where you've located the carpet size–estimating tool, if there are psychological reasons users don't want to use an online calculator to estimate their carpet, and how you might address this both with the location of the tool and how you educate users on the availability and functionality of the tool. You might solve the problem with a simple relabeling of the calculator, or you might find that users don't trust the estimates they receive from an online calculator. You can use the principles discussed in this book to address both of these situations. Chapter 7 on framing communication would help address the relabeling, and chapters 2 and 3 provide guidance on how you can build users' trust using principles of psychology. (Show them others are using the calculator, provide testimonials supporting the calculator's accuracy, and offer a guarantee on the accuracy, for example.)

## 10.2    Choosing the right principle

I've given you seven principles to choose from. You might select one and see how that works, or you might select elements from all seven to include in your design. But how do you know which concept is right for your design? There's no one-size-fits-all answer. Consider the following questions when choosing a principle:

- What are you trying to accomplish beyond usability? All of the principles in this book cover this.
- Is your experience social? Start with something from chapter 6 on social identity and social influence.
- Is your experience intimate or personal? Start with chapter 5 on influence or chapter 8 on persuasion, complemented with framing from chapter 7.
- Are you designing for frequent behaviors such as personal banking or checking the weather forecast? Start with chapter 2 on planned behavior and chapter 4 on presenting effective triggers.
- Are you designing for spontaneous behaviors such as eating out in an unfamiliar neighborhood, or signing up for a monthly newsletter while users are browsing your website for the first time? Start with chapter 3 on risky decisions and chapter 4 on presenting effective triggers.
- Does your experience sell things? Start with chapter 5 on influence and chapter 8 on persuasion.
- Does your experience promote a certain attitude toward a political or environmental issue? Start with chapter 2 on planned behavior.
- Is your experience health or fitness related? Start with chapter 2 on planned behavior, chapter 4 on presenting effective triggers, and chapter 7 on framing communication.

## 10.3 *Making the case for psychology*

You might be suggesting a new approach when you talk about addressing psychological principles in your design. I haven't encountered resistance to the idea. Some people become very excited about the idea of addressing psychology in design, others simply acknowledge that it's something you should address. I haven't experienced resistance to the idea of incorporating these principles, or others from psychology, into the design process. Here are a few speaking points in case you do encounter resistance:

- You become proficient at designing for psychology through education and practice, not spending more money on design tools.
- You can apply psychology across products, across platforms, and across mediums; you'll never lose the need for psychology as long as you design for human use.
- Psychological principles provide a framework or roadmap for how to accomplish your goals of more users using your product the way you intended.

## 10.4 *UX research methods*

I highlighted the importance of conducting research before, during, and after you create your design, throughout this book. I recommend a trained professional researcher to help design, collect data, and analyze data, and report findings and recommendations for each of these methods. Research isn't something anyone can decide to do on a whim. It takes years to become proficient at each method. It takes years to become proficient at making relevant recommendations from the data collected. You do benefit from a working knowledge of user experience research methods, though, so that you can collaborate efficiently and effectively with your researcher.

Here's a description of seven common user-research methods you should be aware of:

- *Competitive and comparative analysis*—Competitive and comparative analysis involves examination of the digital properties of other organizations (such as websites, smartphone apps, and online account-opening workflows) with the intention of determining the state of the field (competitive) as well as best practices across industries (comparative). I've done competitive and comparative analysis for bank clients in which we looked at how other banks enroll new online customers (we chose top U.S. banks and competitors identified by the client), and then we looked at how popular web properties like LinkedIn, TurboTax, and Twitter enroll new users. The findings involve a mix of what others are doing well, what no one is doing well, and where the client has the best chance to gain an edge.
- *Contextual inquiry*—Contextual inquiry involves interviewing and observing research participants in the setting in which they'd use the product you're testing (the context). The context can range from the office they work in if you're testing business software, to how they'd withdraw money from an ATM at a

bank. Contextual inquiry produces a large amount of data and can be costly if your users are located in hard-to-reach locations. You'll often have pictures and video recordings of the context, audio and screen recordings of the interview, and artifacts such as documents containing schedules or frequently used forms to review. The findings reflect how users are currently accomplishing the task your product will address, how you can best design for the context of use.

- *Card sorting*—Card sorting is a method used to determine how users would logically group content. You should use card sorting to determine what content should fall under your main navigation categories, as well as the relationship users see between content and how they prioritize content. There are a number of free or low-cost online card sorting applications available. You can use your favorite search engine to look for "free card sorting tool.'"

- *Interviews*—Interviews allow you to gain a deep understanding of certain user types. Interviews are intensive and you usually have smaller sample sizes. Interviews allow your researcher to ask critical questions about users' attitudes and behaviors, and follow-up questions to ensure good understanding.

- *Survey*—A survey involves the administration of a questionnaire to your users. These can be open-ended or closed-ended/scaled items. You can measure preferences and attitudes easily with surveys, as well as get large sample sizes for relatively low cost using online survey software, including those available at www.surveygizmo.com, https://www.surveymonkey.com, and www.typeform .com, among others. Your researcher can ask users what parts of your product they find most relevant, what areas they struggle with, what information they need presented and how, as well as who they consider experts on your type of product.

- *Usability testing*—Usability testing is a staple method for UX design practice. Usability testing involves taking your design out and testing it with users. You can achieve valuable insight with as few as five users testing your design if you're willing to test frequently. You'll need to work with your researcher to define what elements of your design you want to test. Are you testing how users will enroll in your product, whether a workflow for making a payment is clear, or where users expect to navigate to if they want to find out how to locate your customer service email address? You should be liberal with usability testing throughout the design cycle. Note that I call it *usability* testing, not user testing. You're testing your design, not the users. If the users fail to complete a task, it's because your design is failing.

- *UX assessment*—A UX assessment (also referred to as heuristic evaluation) evaluates a digital product based on predefined usability best practices. Typically a researcher or usability expert will use a checklist to review a website, portal, or intranet and grade the property on whether or not it meets each item on the assessment. You might have a product meant to help users file their taxes. One item on the assessment might be to use jargon-free language when discussing taxes with users. Your researcher would then review the application to determine whether it meets, misses, or exceeds this standard. UX assessments are a great way to get a baseline reading of where your design is doing well and where it could be improved. You can identify and prioritize areas of improvement based on the results of the assessment.

## 10.5 Measuring impact

We've covered a number of techniques meant to improve your design's current and future performance. You and your design team will want to know if the principles you address are working. Here are four techniques used to measure the impact of your design improvements:

- *Increase in system usability scale (SUS) scores*—The SUS is a ten-question survey given to users after they've engaged with your design. The SUS is used to measure the perceived learnability and usability of a design. You can take multiple measurements using the SUS to see whether a design is becoming more usable through iteration. For example, try giving users the SUS before and after a design change based on one of the principles in this book. For more information on the SUS, see the additional resources.

- *Task completion/conversion*—You should see a greater increase in task completion or conversion if you apply the principles in this book and iterate on your design over time. If you run a website dedicated to spreading the word on a political topic, you should see more users spending longer periods of time browsing, eventually completing a task such as providing you with an email address to send them your newsletter. If you run an e-commerce site, sales should increase. If you distribute information about industry best practices, newsletter subscriptions should increase. If you run a social media site, discussions, sharing, and liking posts should increase. If you run a search engine, searches should increase.

- *Calls to service and topic of calls*—Your design enhancements should address issues that drive calls, emails, and chat with customer service. You should see a decrease in overall service calls if your design enhancements are effective (after the initial bump in calls that can coincide with a redesign). You should also see a shift in call topics—fewer calls related to the issue you've addressed with your design.

- *Return on investment (ROI)*—Determining the ROI is a common tactic to measure the benefit of an investment of resources. Business and marketing fields frequently attempt to measure ROI to examine the value of an upgraded piece of equipment (faster computers for a business) or marketing campaign (purchasing internet and television advertisements for a new product release). I recommend using a professional researcher or statistician to determine your ROI. You'll need to account for the cost of time invested in learning and applying the design changes, and the gain in user efficiency, purchasing, or other desired activity. The basic formula for ROI is (gain from investment − cost of investment)/cost of investment. I've included more information on calculating ROI in the additional resources.

## 10.6   *Talking the talk: your turn to discuss principles of psychology*

I'd like you to complete this final "talking the talk" section as part of the end-of-chapter exercise.

- *Idea conceptualization*—How would you communicate the use of a psychological principle to justify the need for your design idea? Think about your business case (how you'd convince others your design is needed), what your design is meant to address, and how you're using psychology to determine how you'll meet users' needs.
- *Choosing the right principle*—How would you communicate your choice of psychological principle(s) used to inform your design? Think about how you'd tell someone why you chose to address one of the principles in this book. Think about how you'd tell someone you chose *not* to address one of the principles in this book.
- *Conducting research*—How would you communicate the need to conduct research with users to inform how you address psychological principles with your design? Think about what you need to know about users to effectively address the psychological principles in your design. Think about what type of research is most appropriate to gather this information.
- *Measuring effectiveness*—How would you communicate assessing the success of addressing psychological principles with your design? Think about what you'd like to assess. Think about what type of assessment you'd conduct to gather this information.

## 10.7   *End-of-chapter exercise: which principle is best for your design?*

You've now completed an entire book on psychological principles. Answer the following questions to help identify the principles you'd like to begin using as soon as possible.

1   Which principles, if any, are you currently addressing in your design?

2   Which principle do you think you'd enjoy focusing on the most? Why?

3   What's the purpose of users engaging with your design (e-commerce, social media, information)?

4   Which principle(s) does section 10.2 suggest starting with?

5 Use the space below to sketch or discuss how you might address the principle from the question above in your design.

6 Which principle do you think you'd enjoy focusing on the least? Why?

**Bonus:** Pick one area of your design and try redesigning it using each principle. Use the pieces you like best from each design to create the ultimate psychological design.

## 10.8  *Additional resources*

Brooke, J. (1996). SUS—A quick and dirty usability scale. *Usability Evaluation in Industry*, 189(194), 4–7. (Brooke discusses the creation and application of the system usability scale, including how to score the results.)

Kaushal, R., A.K. Jha, C. Franz, J. Glaser, K.D. Shetty, T. Jaggi, et al. and Brigham and Women's Hospital CPOE Working Group. (2006). Return on investment for a computerized physician order entry system. *Journal of the American Medical Informatics Association*, 13(3), 261–266. (Researchers report the results of a study to determine the return on investment of a computerized physician ordering system.)

Krug, S. (2014). *Don't make me think, revisited: A common sense approach to web usability*. San Francisco, CA: New Riders Publishing. (Krug's seminal work on usability. A must-have for those in UX design.)

Nielsen, J. (1999). Designing web usability: The practice of simplicity. San Francisco, CA: New Riders Publishing. (Jacob Nielson's guide to designing for web usability. He provides insight into how to design to quickly connect with users.)

Phillips, P. P. and J.J. Phillips. (2009.) Return on investment, in *Handbook of Improving Performance in the Workplace: Volumes* 1-3 (eds. K. H. Silber, W. R. Foshay, R. Watkins, D. Leigh, J. L. Moseley, and J. C. Dessinger), pp. 823–846. Hoboken, NJ: John Wiley & Sons, Inc. (Researchers describe a method of calculating return on investment using 10 steps. The authors discuss the use of return on investment to evaluate a project's success.)

Sauro, J., & J.R. Lewis. (2012). Quantifying the user experience: Practical statistics for user research. Waltham, MA: Elsevier. (Sauro and Lewis provide guidelines for conducting quantitative research on user experience.)

Spencer, D. (2009). Card sorting: Designing usable categories. New York: Rosenfeld Media. http://rosenfeldmedia.com/books/card-sorting/. (Spencer provides a how-to for conducting card sorting as a research method.)

KEYWORDS: return on investment (ROI), system usability scale, user experience research, usability testing

## 10.9   *Summary*

- You can include psychological principles at each phase of designing a product.
- You should discuss with clients, peers, and users, in jargon-free terms, how you've used principles of psychology to inform your process.
- You should engage in user research to inform how you address psychological principles in your design.
- Competitive/comparative analysis, card sorting, contextual inquiry, interviews, surveys, usability testing, and UX assessment are frequently used UX research methods.
- You can measure the effectiveness of your design and design updates using a variety of methods, including the system usability scale, task completion, calls to service, and return on investment.

# *index*

# RELATED MANNING TITLES

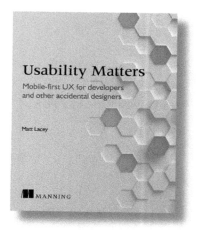

### Usability Matters
by Matt Lacey

ISBN 9781617293931
392 pages, $44.99
July 2018

### CSS in Depth
by Keith J. Grant
Foreword by Chris Coyier

ISBN 9781617293450
472 pages, $44.99
March 2018

### Web Design Playground
by Paul McFedries

ISBN 9781617294402
440 pages, $39.99
April 2019

*For ordering information go to www.manning.com*